EXERCISE YOUR MIND

mind STRETCHERS

INDIGO EDITION

MORE THAN 350 CROSSWORDS, LOGIC PUZZLES, WORDSEARCHES, CODEWORDS AND BRAINTEASERS

Reader's Digest

Published by The Reader's Digest Association, Inc.
London • New York • Sydney • Montreal

Dear Puzzler,

Welcome to the new edition of *Mind Stretchers*. By now, I'd imagine our regular readers are getting to grips with the intricacies and quirks of many of the different puzzles and brainteasers. But if you have been sticking to tried and tested favourites, and flicking quickly past unfamiliar challenges, now is the time to spread your puzzle wings. In this edition we set the spotlight on a perfect puzzle for those who usually blanch at the sight of sudoku and other logical grid puzzles. The puzzle in question is Find the Ships, which features in our masterclass.

The beauty for me of Find the Ships is that it puts a new spin on the classic pencil-and-paper game of Battleships, a favourite from my childhood. Many of the simplest puzzles and games stand the test of time, and this particular game is still popular, whether on paper or as a console game. In the version I used to play, each of two players would mark the locations of the ships in their 'fleet' on a grid, taking care not to let their opponent see. The fleet of ships would comprise battleships, cruisers, destroyers, aircraft carriers and submarines, or whatever else was desired. The larger the ship, the more squares on the grid it would occupy. The players would then take turns to guess a square of the grid in which an opponent's ship might be located by giving a grid reference for the square. If indeed there was a ship on that square, the ship would be declared hit. When all the squares corresponding to a ship had been hit, the ship was sunk. Whichever player's ships were all sunk first, lost the game.

For all the hours of fun I had from this game all those years ago, it was essentially a game of chance. A knowledge of your opponent might give you a clue to where their ships would be lurking, but winning or losing was literally hit or miss. Despite looking and feeling similar to Battleships, this is where Find the Ships blows the original game out of the water. In the puzzle version in these pages, your opponent is the setter, the ships are in place, and solving the puzzle depends on logic, not luck.

I hope I've whetted your appetite for Find the Ships if it's a puzzle you've not tried before. Follow our step-by-step guide on pages 4-5, and you'll soon be going full steam ahead. And while we're on the subject of ships, it seems fitting to mention the Brain Breather on page 194, which explores the influence of our seafaring heritage on the English language.

Happy puzzling!

George Rankin

George Rankin
Editor

★★★★★ Star Gazing

Each of the main puzzles has been given a star rating. This gives an idea of the puzzle's difficulty, from one star to the trickiest five-star puzzles. It's just a general guideline. You may find individual puzzles or puzzle types easier than others.

Contents

Puzzle Masterclass: FIND THE SHIPS

Find the Ships is based on the classic pencil-and-paper game of Battleships. The object of both the game and the puzzle is to discover the positions of ships on a grid diagram, but there the similarities end. Whereas the original game is an exercise in trial and error, the puzzle is a logical challenge, containing all the information needed to solve it. As with all the best logic puzzles, Find the Ships comes in varying standards of difficulty and you won't need to work in Naval Intelligence to enjoy it.

THE PUZZLE

A fleet of ten ships of varying sizes must be positioned in a grid which represents an area of ocean. Each ship will occupy between one and four squares of the grid, depending on its type.

Know your fleet. The different types and sizes of ship are shown here.

Aircraft carrier:
Battleship:
Cruiser:
Destroyer:

An aircraft carrier has four sections, and occupies four squares of the grid, a battleship takes up three squares, a cruiser two squares and a destroyer just one square. In most versions of the puzzle (including all of those in this edition) there are four destroyers, three cruisers, two battleships and one aircraft carrier to position. We've named the types of ship in the masterclass to help in explanation, but these names are often omitted from the puzzles.

Numbers at the edge of the grid indicate how many squares in that row or column contain parts of ships. At the start of the puzzle, some information may also be given within the grid. Some squares may be marked with parts of ships. Other squares may be marked with wavy lines. These indicate water and will not contain part of a ship.

THE RULES

The ships must be positioned horizontally or vertically (never diagonally) in the grid, and no two of them will touch each other, not even diagonally. In other words

each ship will be separated from the others by squares of water.

THE FIRST STEPS

Begin the puzzle by using all the information you've been given. How you mark this information is your choice, but here's what I do. I mark squares that represent sea (with no parts of ships) with a cross. If I know that a square contains part of a ship, but do not know which part it is, which type of ship it belongs to or in which direction the rest of the ship lies, then I mark the square with a small dot.

A sensible first step is to look for any row or column that is marked with a 0. This contains no parts of ships, so you can immediately mark every square in the row or column with a cross.

Next, consider any parts of ships that have been entered as starters. The shape of each part will determine how much information you can glean from it. If a single-square destroyer is given, you know that each square surrounding it can be marked with a cross, as it must contain sea.

If the part is a semicircular end part, you can tell which way the ship is oriented and therefore mark one adjacent square with a dot to signify part of a ship that could either be a semicircular end part

or a square centre part. You can also mark sea in all but one of the squares surrounding these two.

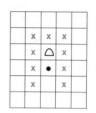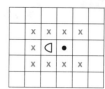

If a given starter part is a square centre section of a ship, you will not necessarily know whether the ship lies horizontally or vertically, so will have to wait until you eliminate one of the directions before marking any further squares.

Once you have entered all the available information in the grid, compare the numbers of ship parts listed beside the rows and below the columns with everything you have marked in the grid to see if anything new can be deduced. For instance, any rows and columns that already have their quota of ship parts can be completed with crosses. Look too for any rows and columns that have their quota of sea squares, and must therefore be completed with parts of ships.

Another useful approach to solving is to look for potential locations for the larger ships. It should be possible, quite early in the solving, to eliminate all but a handful of locations for the four-square aircraft carrier.

Remember to cross off the ships on the reference list as you position them in the grid. Now follow the steps of our example puzzle.

EXAMPLE PUZZLE

Follow our step-by-step guide to solve the puzzle below. We've marked the columns A to K and the rows 1 to 10 to make the explanations easier to follow.

diagram 1

	A	B	C	D	E	F	G	H	J	K	
1								≈			2
2											0
3								□			4
4											1
5											1
6								□			2
7											1
8	≈										1
9											7
10											1
	5	0	2	0	2	1	2	3	1	4	

Diagram 1 shows the initial puzzle grid, with two squares of water, and two parts of ships already marked as starters.

The first step, marked on diagram 2, is to put an X (for empty sea) in every square of every row or column that is marked with a zero. Squares 2A to 2K must be empty. So are B1 to B10 and D1 to D10.

Marking the X in H2 means that the ship whose middle section is in H3 cannot go down the H column, so it must lie along row 3. So we know G3 and J3 contain ship parts, but we don't yet know what type of ship.

diagram 2

	A	B	C	D	E	F	G	H	J	K	
1		X		X				≈	X		2
2	X	X	X	X	X	X	X	X	X	X	0
3		X		X		●	□	●			4
4		X		X	X	X	X	X	X		1
5		X		X				X	△		1
6		X		X				X	□		2
7		X		X				X	●		1
8	≈	X		X				X			1
9		X		X				X			7
10		X		X				X			1
	5	0	2	0	2	1	2	3	1	4	

Column J is marked with a 1, so the ship's part in J3 is the only one in that column, and the remaining squares can be marked with an X. As that ship must be surrounded by water, we can put Xs in F4, G4, H4 and K4.

The section of ship in K6 is a middle part, so K5 must be an end part. But we don't know yet if this is the aircraft carrier or a battleship, so what type of part goes in K7 is still uncertain.

Turning now to diagram 3, we can see that high numbers can be as useful as the zeros. Row 9 has a 7 by it. We've already marked three squares as empty, so the rest must all be occupied. This row must contain the aircraft carrier. As there must be empty water around the aircraft carrier, E8-H8 and E10-H10 can be crossed off. The vessel previously marked in column K must be a battleship, so K8 must be empty. The ship in row 3 must also be a battleship, so F3 and K3 can be marked as empty.

diagram 3

	A	B	C	D	E	F	G	H	J	K	
1		X	X	X				≈	X	X	2
2	X	X	X	X	X	X	X	X	X	X	0
3		X	X	X		X	◁	□	▷	X	4
4		X	X	X		X	X	X	X	X	1
5		X	X	X				X	△		1
6		X	X	X				X	□		2
7		X	X	X				X	▽		1
8	≈	X	△	X	X	X	X	X	X	X	1
9	●	X	▽	X	◁	□	□	▷	X	◯	7
10		X	X	X	X	X	X	X	X	X	1
	5	0	2	0	2	1	2	3	1	4	

Row 8 has one ship part and only C8 is available, so that can be filled. There are only two ship parts in column C, so C8-9 must contain a cruiser, and the rest of that column can be crossed off. Column K has all four parts required, so there must be a destroyer in K9, and the remaining squares can be marked as empty.

Moving on to diagram 4 we see that rows 5 and 7 also have their full complement of ship parts, so can be completed with Xs. Row 10 has one ship part and only A10 is available, so that is filled and we have located a second cruiser.

Columns F and G both have their quota of parts, so the other squares in these columns can be marked as empty. Column H needs a third ship part and only H6 is available, so that is the site of one of the destroyers. This in turn means that row 6 has the two parts specified, so A6 and E6 must be empty.

We have located a two-part cruiser in column A, so the column needs three more parts to be complete. A1, A3 and A4 must therefore be filled, giving us another destroyer and the third cruiser. E4 must be empty as row 4 already has its one section and E3 is empty as row 3 is complete. This means that E1 must contain a destroyer to complete row 1. The full solution is now in place.

diagram 4

	A	B	C	D	E	F	G	H	J	K	
1	◯	X	X	X	◯	X	X	≈	X	X	2
2	X	X	X	X	X	X	X	X	X	X	0
3	△	X	X	X	X	X	◁	□	▷	X	4
4	▽	X	X	X	X	X	X	X	X	X	1
5	X	X	X	X	X	X	X	X	△		1
6	X	X	X	X	X	X	X	◯	X	□	2
7	X	X	X	X	X	X	X	X	▽		1
8	≈	X	△	X	X	X	X	X	X	X	1
9	△	X	▽	X	◁	□	□	▷	X	◯	7
10	▽	X	X	X	X	X	X	X	X	X	1
	5	0	2	0	2	1	2	3	1	4	

Now turn the page to put the masterclass theory into practice. There are 10 Find the Ships puzzles of varying difficulty throughout this edition, starting on page 6.

★ Find the Ships

Determine the position of the 10 ships listed on the right of the grid; one piece has been inserted in the grid to get you started. The ships may be oriented either horizontally or vertically. A square with wavy lines indicates water and will not contain part of a ship. The numbers at the edge of the grid indicate how many squares in that row or column contain parts of ships. When all 10 ships are correctly placed in the grid, no two of them will touch each other, not even diagonally. You'll find tips for solving this puzzle in our masterclass on pages 4-5.

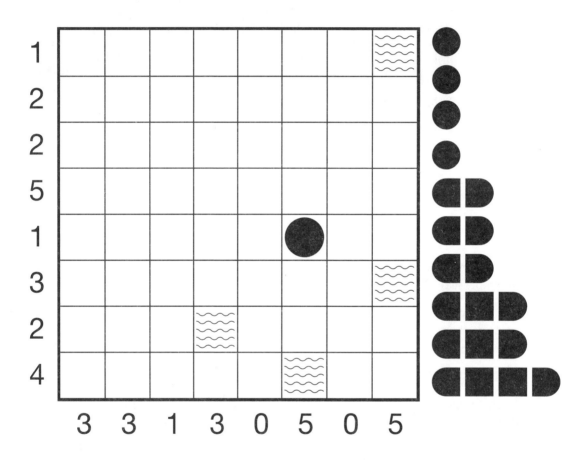

BETWEENER

What five-letter word can be inserted between the two words below to make a well-known expression with each?

Example: SWEET _ _ _ _ _ PICK
Answer: TOOTH – sweet tooth, toothpick

GLOSS __ __ __ __ __ BRUSH

★★ Codeword

Can you crack the code and complete the grid? Each letter of the alphabet appears at least once in the grid, and is represented by the same number throughout. The letters we've decoded should help you to identify other letters and words in the grid.

	26	18	19	7	6	2	■	3	6	7	18	7	5	■
24	■	5	■	21		6	24	17		5	■	16	■	6
3	6	8	14	16	7	6	■	4	12	17	17	23	6	2
17	■	12	■	18		2	■	■	8	■	23	■	18	
19	13	9	17	13	6	■	15	19	8	11	26	17	17	5
13	■	■	5	■	■		5	■	9	■	3	■		
18	13	1	14	6	10	18	26	14	6	■	7	5	19	24
13	■	17	■	2	■	20	■	19	■	18	■	6	■	19
24	3	16	26	■	8	17	13	7	18	2	6	3	6	2
■	■	13	■	19	■	3	■	■		6	■			24
7	18	2	6	4	19	9	7	■	22	17	25	26	18	6
17	■	14	■	19	■	■		19	■	14	■	18	■	5
1	3	18	7	11	6	2	■	26	3	17	4	7	6	3
5	■	13	■	6	■	3	16	6	■	24	■	17	■	9
■	19	24	6	13	8	9	■	5 T	3 R	9 Y	18	13	24	■

A B C D E F G H I J K L M N O P Q ~~R~~ S ~~T~~ U V W X ~~Y~~ Z

1	2	3 **R**	4	5 **T**	6	7	8	9 **Y**	10	11	12	13
14	15	16	17	18	19	20	21	22	23	24	25	26

★ Four Square

Enter the maze at top left, pass through each of the red squares exactly once, then exit at bottom right. You may not retrace your path.

AND SO ON

Unscramble the letters in the phrase AWARE STOP to form two words that are linked by the word 'and' in a common phrase.

Example: Unscramble the phrase LEATHER HAY
Answer: HALE and HEARTY

—————————— and ——————————

★ Wordsearch – The Big Cheese

Find the 21 listed types of cheese that are hidden in the grid. They may read horizontally, vertically or diagonally, and either backwards or forwards.

Bavarian
Boursin
Brie
Camembert
Cheddar
Cheshire
Derby
Edam
Emmental
Feta
Gouda
Gruyere
Halloumi
Havarti
Jarlsberg
Leerdammer
Parmesan
Pecorino
Ricotta
Roquefort
Stilton

Q	K	F	J	H	A	L	L	O	U	M	I	L	D	O
U	V	E	A	E	A	D	Y	O	Q	B	L	A	Y	U
T	A	T	R	P	J	V	H	N	R	E	T	T	G	R
Y	F	A	L	R	R	O	A	I	E	G	V	N	T	Z
B	B	M	S	G	O	K	E	R	I	H	S	E	H	C
U	S	R	B	W	L	Q	D	O	T	T	G	M	R	K
N	F	S	E	N	R	A	U	C	R	I	R	M	A	M
O	A	C	R	D	M	A	K	E	J	X	U	E	L	B
T	S	S	G	M	T	A	B	P	F	I	Y	O	O	W
L	C	I	E	T	P	M	I	X	W	O	E	U	P	E
I	X	R	O	M	E	E	B	A	V	A	R	I	A	N
T	Z	C	F	M	R	D	D	H	N	S	E	T	U	V
S	I	B	A	H	N	A	Q	A	I	G	O	U	D	A
R	B	C	C	M	D	G	P	N	M	E	B	W	X	N
R	A	D	D	E	H	C	S	F	J	Z	Y	L	A	C

INITIAL REACTION

The words of a well-known proverb or saying have been reduced to their initial letters. Can you restore the missing words?

Example: B I T T W
Answer: **Blood Is Thicker Than Water**

L B Y L _____

★ Sudoku

Fill in all the empty cells in the grid so that each row, each column and each 3x3 block contains all the digits from 1-9.

		9			4	7		
		6		1	7		4	
2	4			3		9		1
					8		1	9
	7	1				4	5	
6	9		3					
7		4		2			3	6
	2		4	6		5		
		3	8			1		

MAKE TRACKS

Lay the 'sleepers' of the track by writing the answers to the clues in the numbered Down spaces. Then work out the two 'rail' answers, reading across. The 'rail' answers, which are not necessarily single words, are items of fruit and vegetables.

1 Of the Sun
2 Fruit-flavoured party dessert
3 Float without steering
4 Be too inquisitive
5 Trusty horse

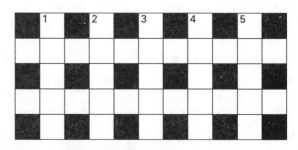

★★ Crossword

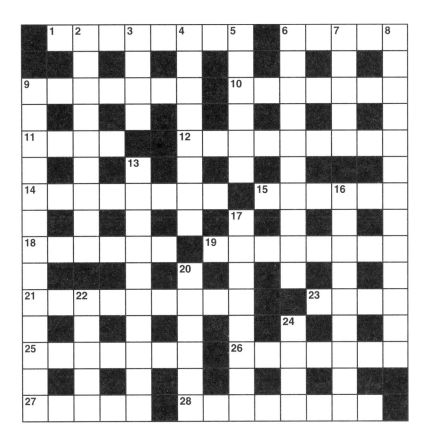

ACROSS

1 Not corrected (text) (8)

6 Design added to a garment (5)

9 Combat aircraft (7)

10 National fund-raising raffle (7)

11 Ballet dancer's short stiff skirt (4)

12 Spiny marine creature (3,6)

14 Envisaged (8)

15 Optimistic (6)

18 Incidents (6)

19 In classical mythology, food of the gods (8)

21 Stomach upset (9)

23 Dull throbbing pain (4)

25 Prospect (7)

26 Mimic, copy (7)

27 Land of the Pharaohs (5)

28 US cattle-farm owners (8)

DOWN

2 Settle by discussion (9)

3 Tax on goods (4)

4 Machine for separating grain from corn (8)

5 Australian currency unit (6)

6 Activity such as Formula One racing (5,5)

7 Dentures (5)

8 Acrobat's circus swing (6,7)

9 Be the right size and well suited (3,4,1,5)

13 Person who drops rubbish all over the place (6,4)

16 Comfy seat (4,5)

17 Exclusion (8)

20 Bram ___, author of *Dracula* (6)

22 Asian peanut sauce (5)

24 Plate, bowl (4)

★ Fences

Connect adjacent dots with vertical or horizontal lines, so that a single loop with no crossings or branches is formed in the grid. Each number indicates how many lines surround it. Square spaces with no number may be surrounded by any number of lines.

```
2 1 3      2 0 1
  1   1
                    2
  1 2 3    2
        3    2 3 3
    0
             1   3
  3 2 0      2 3 2
```

ADDITION SWITCH

Switch the positions of two of the digits in this incorrect sum to make a calculation that works.

Example: 955 + 264 = 411
Answer: 155 + 264 = 419 (switch the 9 in 955 with the second 1 in 411)

$$
\begin{array}{r}
1\ 6\ 8 \\
+\ 5\ 0\ 6 \\
\hline
2\ 3\ 4
\end{array}
$$

★★ Line Drawing

Draw three straight lines, each from one edge of the square to another edge, to create four regions, each one containing letters that combine to spell a word of a different length from the others.

```
E        N              H
             I         A

  A
        R                 T
                 A
                            E
     S       U
               E            I


  E    T
           R                  E
```

ALTER EGO

Solve the anagram contained in the bold capital letters of the clue to find the name of a celebrity. Do you know their real name?

Example: **CUSTOMER I** mistake for this Top Gun
Answer: **TOM CRUISE. His real name was Thomas Mapother IV**

No **JUDE LAW SIREN** – she was a singing nun!

★ Wordsearch – Castles

Find the 22 listed castles that are hidden in the grid. They may read horizontally, vertically or diagonally, and either backwards or forwards.

Alnwick
Arundel
Balmoral
Beaumaris
Berwick
Bodiam
Caernarfon
Caister
Chepstow
Conwy
Corfe
Deal
Dover
Dudley
Edinburgh
Hastings
Hever
Leeds
Pevensey
Tintagel

Walmer
Warwick

Y	A	D	O	V	E	R	C	E	Z	G	Z	E	L	E
W	R	E	M	L	A	W	D	H	C	Q	F	B	E	B
N	U	K	L	W	D	I	B	B	E	R	W	I	C	K
O	N	C	I	A	N	V	E	Y	O	P	N	U	K	Y
C	D	I	H	B	R	M	A	C	E	O	S	J	D	B
W	E	W	U	E	K	O	U	T	F	L	R	T	O	S
R	L	R	N	Y	V	M	M	R	D	E	D	D	O	J
W	G	A	C	E	J	E	A	L	T	O	I	U	U	W
H	L	W	L	S	X	N	R	S	A	A	P	Y	D	Y
N	E	S	I	N	R	X	I	O	M	B	N	F	O	P
H	E	Q	F	E	W	A	S	G	N	I	T	S	A	H
R	D	D	A	V	C	I	A	S	E	Y	D	L	H	P
Q	S	C	Z	E	T	K	C	B	X	E	Z	I	H	A
U	V	A	X	P	F	N	T	K	A	V	M	C	M	B
T	I	N	T	A	G	E	L	L	G	G	R	L	U	H

BRAINSTRETCHER

Choose the lettered answer that best copies the pattern of the first link. Some lateral thinking is required.

Example: *fence* is to *sword*, as *vault* is to: (a) jump (b) pole (c) arch
Answer: POLE. You vault with a pole, just as you fence with a sword.

underscore is to *stress*, as *underpin* is to:

(a) support (b) ensure (c) overstress (d) undo

★★ Number Jig

Fit all the listed numbers into the grid. One number is already in place to help you get started.

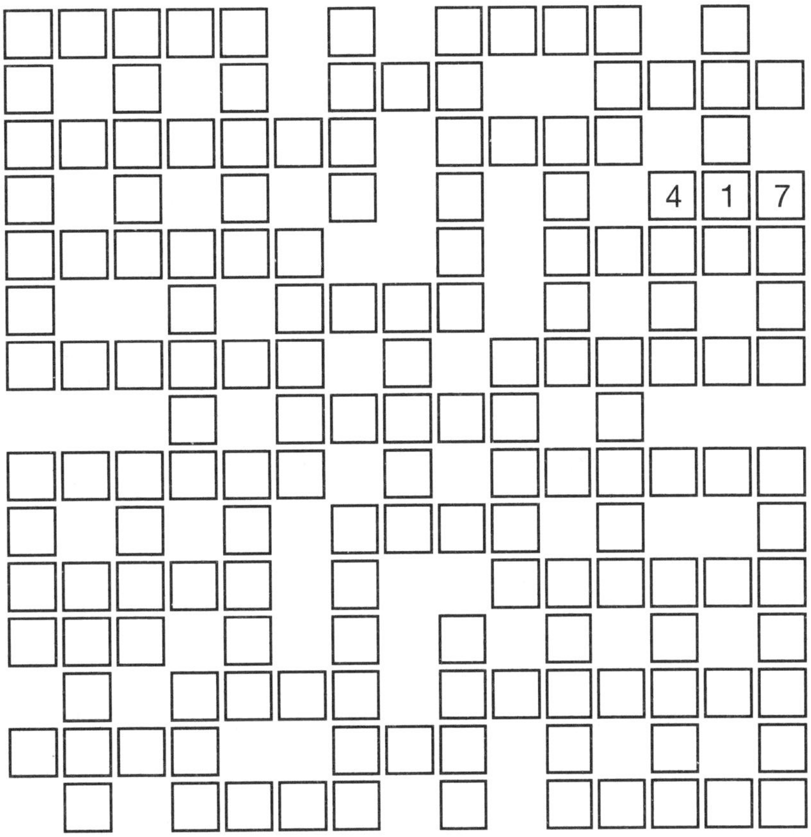

3 digits

101
~~417~~
816
820
920
975

4 digits

1239
1430
1853
1956
2042
3341
4551
4657
5841
6047
7452
8731
8765
9834

5 digits

13296
20803
21075
24613
30758
31677
33432
33434
41647
42248
54404
55287
66634
77574
78567
85773
88068
91261

6 digits

101361
478702
626542
657736
723700
885756
946597
978741

7 digits

2294966
6200044
9302580
9504445

★★ Codeword

Can you crack the code and complete the grid? Each letter of the alphabet appears at least once in the grid, and is represented by the same number throughout. The letters we've decoded should help you to identify other letters and words in the grid.

4	23	6	23	25	9		23	8	2	21		15	14	17
2		25		17		15		4		25		14		25
21	12	17	17	2	9	9	23	23		1	12	26	26	18
6		17		15		4		15		21		16		26
	26	12	7	15	25	2		15	20	14	23	23	11	23
21		21				13				1		21		
6	2	19	23	13		23	10	9	4	25	21	9	23	13
										A	C	T		
25			23		7		25		9				14
8	25	4	25	15	2	9	2	21		23	10	8	23	1
		25		23				9			1		18
24	6	2	4	4	23	13		1	25	4	5	23	4	
6		1		9		4		23		14		7		15
25	1	2	26	2		12	26	15	23	4	3	25	7	9
1		7		12		24		15		25		4		14
23	5	5		7	12	7	23		22	1	25	18	23	13

A B C̸ D E F G H I J K L M N O P Q R S T̸ U V W X Y Z

1	2	3	4	5	6	7	8	9 T	10	11	12	13
14	15	16	17	18	19	20	21 C	22	23	24	25 A	26

★★ Killer Sudoku

As in regular sudoku, fill all the empty cells in the grid so that each row, each column and each 3x3 block contains all the digits from 1-9. In addition, the digits in each dotted-line shape must add up to the number given in the top left corner of the shape, and no digit may be repeated within each dotted shape.

12		6		14		16	4	
7		17		3			13	17
15		6		23	7			
3	11				15		8	
	16				8			5
12	5	17	8		17	6	16	
				12				20
22		4			6	10		
	8		11			5		

RHYMING TRIO

Rearrange the listed letters to form three one-syllable words that rhyme.

Example:	A A A B C E K S W X X
Answer:	AXE, BACKS, WAX

A A A C C C H K K M T W

_____   _____   _____

★★ Skeleton Crossword

FULL
SYMMETRY
PATTERN

Using the clue numbers and black squares already in the grid to get you started, fill in the black squares as well as the answers to complete this crossword. The grid follows a fully symmetrical pattern.

ACROSS

1 External direction
5 Pertaining to the stomach
9 Adam's partner
10 Personal teacher
11 Needless
12 Version of a book
13 Lose body fluid
15 Regarding
17 Calm
20 Person ruling in place of another
22 Inequitable
24 Aid to drawing a straight line
25 ___ Borealis, Northern Lights
26 Smeared
28 Throw
31 Group of concubines
34 Disc used in place of money
36 Pungent chemical used in smelling salts
37 Liable to sulk
38 Cost of an item
39 Nervous twitch
40 Merit, earn
41 Doctor who performs operations

DOWN

1 Tenth month of the year
2 Name of a book
3 Ventilated

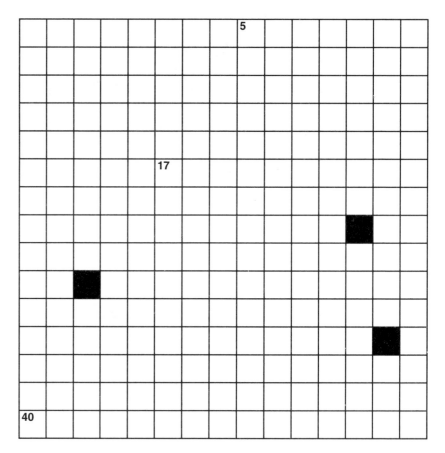

4 Show
5 Amiable, cheerful
6 Finnish steam bath
7 Wireless
8 Originator
14 Blot on the landscape
16 American bison
17 Thin leather band
18 Creek, small bay
19 Move forward suddenly
21 Australian flightless bird
23 Anger

25 Humiliated
27 Castle jail
29 Prisoner
30 Sceptics
32 Beginnings
33 Civic leader
34 Become thinner at one end
35 Weapon with a blade

★★ One-Way Streets

The diagram represents a pattern of streets. A and B are parking spaces, and the black squares are shops. Find the route that starts at A, passes through all the shops exactly once, and ends at B. Arrows indicate one-way traffic for that block only. No block or intersection may be entered more than once.

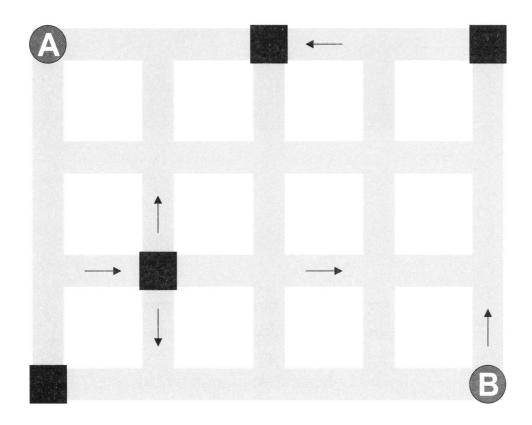

LOGICAL

See if you can solve this mini logic problem in your head before writing anything down.

Three motorists set off for London to see who could get there first, one travelling by motorbike, one by car and one in a van. Each kept to one type of road, either A-roads, B-roads or motorways. The car went via B-roads and didn't finish last. The vehicle travelling on the A-roads finished first. If the van arrived after the car, what type of vehicle reached London first?

★★ Out of Order

The order of the six lettered blocks has been altered. From the information given, work out what positions the blocks now occupy.

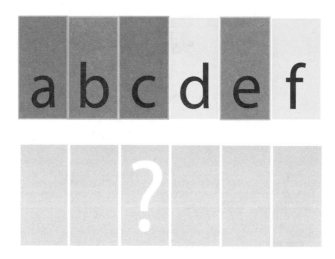

The far right-hand block is now green.

The yellow blocks are positioned in alphabetical order.

The vowels are together.

The c is between two orange blocks.

CHOP AND CHANGE

Delete one letter from the word **DOUBLES** and rearrange the rest to get an article of clothing.

Example: Delete one letter from **CHECKERS** and rearrange the rest to get a blood-curdling sound.

Answer: **SCREECH (drop the K)**

★★ Star Search

Find the stars that are hidden in some of the blank squares. The numbered squares indicate how many stars are hidden in the squares adjacent to them (including diagonally). There is never more than one star in any square.

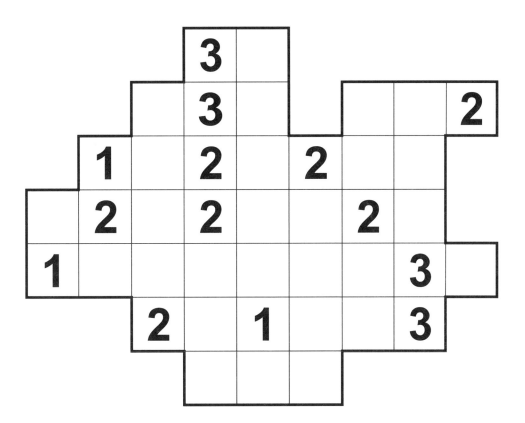

TELEPHONE TRIOS

Using the numbers and letters on the telephone keypad, what three seven-letter words, names or phrases on a common theme can be formed from the numbers below?

3547326   __ __ __ __ __ __ __

7422776   __ __ __ __ __ __ __

8264644   __ __ __ __ __ __ __

1	ABC 2	DEF 3
GHI 4	JKL 5	MNO 6
PRS 7	TUV 8	WXY 9
*	0	#

★★★ Killer Sudoku

As in regular sudoku, fill all the empty cells in the grid so that each row, each column and each 3x3 block contains all the digits from 1-9. In addition, the digits in each dotted-line shape must add up to the number given in the top left corner of the shape, and no digit may be repeated within each dotted shape.

5		22			5		13	
12	22	9	5		20		21	
			21	13				5
				7				
22	19		19			13		16
				11		7		
	7	3	14		8	14		
			26			13	5	12
13				3				

INITIAL REACTION

The words of a well-known proverb or saying have been reduced to their initial letters. Can you restore the missing words?

H W H I L _____

★★ Crossword

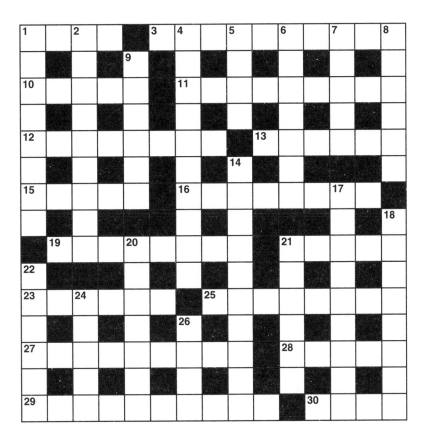

ACROSS

1 Fruit which, when dried, is a prune (4)

3 Thumbed a lift (5-5)

10 1983 film directed by and starring Barbra Streisand (5)

11 Have a good time (4,5)

12 Declined to take part (5,3)

13 Feeling of having had the same experience before (4,2)

15 Small island in the Inner Hebrides (5)

16 Part of a vehicle closest to the kerb (8)

19 Grace, refinement (8)

21 Spanish word for 'friend' (5)

23 On a ship or plane (6)

25 Nauseated, or took to the streets (8)

27 Over the moon, thrilled (4-1-4)

28 ___ Campbell, supermodel (5)

29 All around (10)

30 Border, rim (4)

DOWN

1 Historic Devon city and port (8)

2 Artificial (9)

4 Wearing black clothes when someone dies (2,8)

5 Fuel obtained from coal (4)

6 Tools for hitting nails (7)

7 South ___, Seoul's country (5)

8 Rehearsal, practice (3,3)

9 Toboggan (6)

14 Estate's wildlife warden (10)

17 Floating timber (9)

18 Place to dig up a precious metal (4,4)

20 European country, capital Berlin (7)

21 Quantity (6)

22 Socially clumsy and awkward (6)

24 Promptly (2,3)

26 Night-time flying insect (4)

★★ Hyper-Sudoku

Fill in the empty cells so that every row, column, 3x3 block and each of the four 3x3 grey regions contains all of the digits from 1-9.

	1		3	9	6			
	2			7		6	1	
6	9					3		
		3		5	2			4
					9		8	
9	8			3	4			1
5					7		2	6
	4	6			3		9	7
8	7	9				4	3	

AND SO ON

Unscramble the letters in the phrase SCOT SENT KISS to form two words that are linked by the word 'and' in a common phrase.

————————— and —————————

★★ Child's Play

Which of the numbered pictures is the mirrored reflection of the child's painting?

BETWEENER

What three-letter word can be inserted between the two words below to make a well-known expression with each?

FRESH __ __ __ FORCE

★★ 123

Fill each blank square in the grid with the number 1, 2 or 3 so that each completed row and column has an equal number of 1s, 2s and 3s. Each bold rectangular block must contain all three numbers, and no two horizontally or vertically adjacent squares may contain the same number.

			2		
3				**1**	
		3			
				3	

SUDOKU SUM

Write a digit from 0-9 in each of the five blank spaces to make a calculation that works. No digit may be repeated in the sum.

```
   _ 0 _
 + 2 _ 7
 ───────
   _ 5 _
```

★★ Codeword

Can you crack the code and complete the grid? Each letter of the alphabet appears at least once in the grid, and is represented by the same number throughout. The letters we've decoded should help you to identify other letters and words in the grid.

A B C̸ D E F G H I̸ J K L M N O P Q R S T̸ U V W X Y Z

1	2	3	4	5 C	6	7 I	8	9	10	11	12	13
14	15	16 T	17	18	19	20	21	22	23	24	25	26

★ ABC

Enter the letters A, B and C into the diagram so that each row and column has exactly one A, one B and one C, leaving one blank box in each row and column. The letters outside the diagram indicate the first letter encountered, moving in the direction of the arrow.

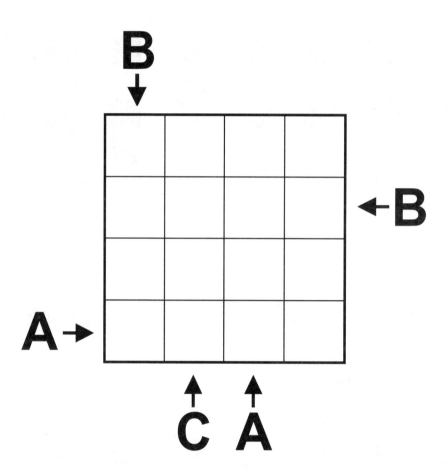

CLUELESS CROSSWORD

Complete the crossword with common seven-letter words, not using names (proper nouns), based entirely on the letters already filled in for you.

★★ Find the Ships

Determine the position of the 10 ships listed on the right of the grid. The ships may be oriented either horizontally or vertically. The numbers at the edge of the grid indicate how many squares in that row or column contain parts of ships. When all 10 ships are correctly placed in the grid, no two of them will touch each other, not even diagonally. You'll find tips for solving this puzzle in our masterclass on pages 4-5.

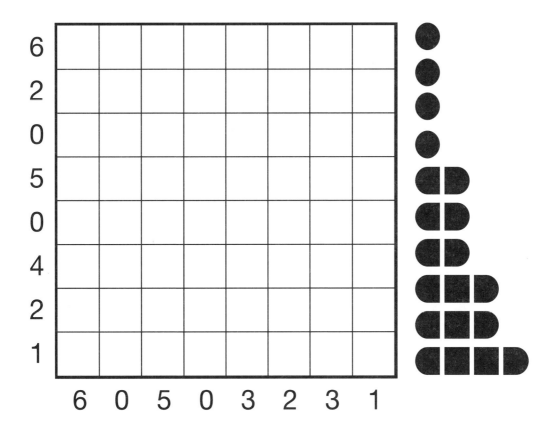

ALTER EGO

Solve the anagram contained in the bold capital letters of the clue to find the name of a celebrity. Do you know their real name?

DISC FLEW to him, My Little Chickadee

★ Wordsearch – Film Genres

Find the 23 listed film genres that are hidden in the grid. They may read horizontally, vertically or diagonally, and either backwards or forwards.

Adventure
Biopic
Bollywood
Buddy
Comedy
Crime
Disaster
Drama
Family
Farce
Film noir
Gangster
Horror
Musical
Mystery
Romance
Romcom
Satire

Slapstick
Sports
Thriller
Western
Zombie

F	Y	Z	I	Z	C	R	C	O	M	E	D	Y	S	Y
G	B	T	O	L	O	E	I	O	K	O	J	I	D	R
P	Q	Q	H	M	W	R	R	E	C	N	M	D	N	E
K	S	P	C	D	B	X	Q	U	I	C	U	H	R	T
R	I	O	N	M	L	I	F	M	T	B	R	E	B	S
T	M	Y	T	C	C	N	E	A	S	N	T	I	V	Y
B	O	L	L	Y	W	O	O	D	P	S	E	L	M	M
J	B	I	S	T	T	G	X	W	A	W	Y	V	U	E
A	I	M	P	H	M	P	A	S	L	J	I	S	D	E
R	O	A	O	R	D	U	I	N	S	S	I	D	C	A
V	P	F	R	I	O	D	V	Z	G	C	F	N	E	D
G	I	H	T	L	E	R	I	T	A	S	A	X	R	B
U	C	K	S	L	E	Y	R	L	K	M	T	A	Z	A
W	E	S	T	E	R	N	Y	O	O	V	M	E	G	L
O	F	E	C	R	A	F	J	R	H	A	U	R	R	B

INITIAL REACTION

The words of a well-known proverb or saying have been reduced to their initial letters. Can you restore the missing words?

W N W N _____

★★ Skeleton Crossword

FULL
SYMMETRY
PATTERN

Using the clue numbers and black squares already in the grid to get you started, fill in the black squares as well as the answers to complete this crossword. The grid follows a fully symmetrical pattern.

ACROSS

- **2** Set forth clearly
- **8** Parasitic insect
- **9** Offspring of a donkey and a horse
- **10** Become liable to
- **11** Indian cotton cloth
- **12** Away from the coast
- **14** Children's magazine
- **15** That is to say, specifically
- **18** Just about
- **21** Team of two
- **23** Linkage
- **24** Secure with a knot
- **25** Hare-brained
- **28** Special ability
- **30** Willing, prepared
- **31** State of being neglected
- **33** Thrusting sword
- **35** Fine porcelain
- **36** ___ *Las Vegas*, 1964 Elvis movie
- **37** Wyatt ___, US lawman
- **38** Venerated

DOWN

- **1** Emotional request
- **2** Sodium chloride solution
- **3** Foolish behaviour
- **4** Unwilling to impart information
- **5** Second-largest continent
- **6** Symbol
- **7** Scottish tribe

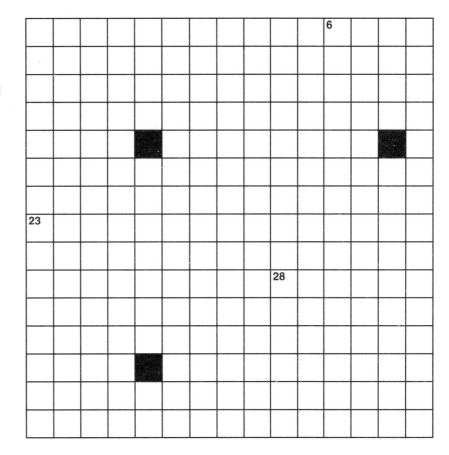

- **11** Verified
- **13** Explosion-triggering device
- **16** Suppressed (sound)
- **17** Caterpillar or grub, eg
- **19** Body-hugging fabric
- **20** ___ Oyl, Popeye's girlfriend
- **21** Tiny mark
- **22** Single integer
- **26** Puma, mountain lion
- **27** Written synopsis
- **28** Despot, dictator
- **29** Became void
- **32** Coloured part of the eye
- **34** Common Continental currency unit

★★ Koala Maze

Enter the maze as indicated, pass through the three yellow dots exactly once, and then exit. You may not retrace your path.

RHYMING TRIO

Rearrange the listed letters to form three one-syllable words that rhyme.

A E E E H I K P R S T

_____   _____   _____

★ Fences

Connect adjacent dots with vertical or horizontal lines, so that a single loop with no crossings or branches is formed in the grid. Each number indicates how many lines surround it. Square spaces with no number may be surrounded by any number of lines.

ADDITION SWITCH

Switch the positions of two of the digits in this incorrect sum to make a calculation that works.

```
   186
 + 379
 ─────
   543
```

★★ Killer Sudoku

As in regular sudoku, fill all the empty cells in the grid so that each row, each column and each 3x3 block contains all the digits from 1-9. In addition, the digits in each dotted-line shape must add up to the number given in the top left corner of the shape, and no digit may be repeated within each dotted shape.

12	4	30	8		18		8	
			23				9	
7				11	20			
10			3		14		20	
21		8		7		15		
		16	14				4	
17				3	11			5
6	13	7			16		23	
		17			5			

AND SO ON

Unscramble the letters in the phrase REBEL SET SKIT to form two words that are linked by the word 'and' in a common phrase.

_____ and _____

★★ Crossword

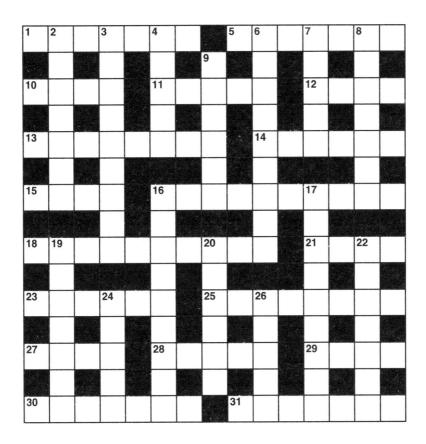

ACROSS

1 End result (7)

5 Opposed to (7)

10 Remnant of a healed wound (4)

11 Stand-offish (5)

12 Heavy grey metal (4)

13 Attractive or encouraging (8)

14 Raw beginner (6)

15 Stained with colour (4)

16 Big feast before Lent (7,3)

18 Voice your thoughts (5,5)

21 Large town (4)

23 Royal house to which Charles I belonged (6)

25 Relating to the arts (8)

27 Sudden fancy (4)

28 Rule of a monarch (5)

29 Burl ___, American actor and ballad-singer (4)

30 Calibre (7)

31 Danger signal (7)

DOWN

2 Spooky, weird (7)

3 Continued, persevered (7,2)

4 Coastal resort and port of Florida (5)

6 Advance, make progress (2,7)

7 House built of ice (5)

8 Physical endurance (7)

9 1986 Tom Cruise film (3,3)

16 Person applying a wall finish (9)

17 Item not covered by an insurance policy (9)

19 Small axe (7)

20 Exotic flower (6)

22 Part-exchange (5,2)

24 Confess (5)

26 Mario ___, opera singer who starred in *The Great Caruso* (5)

★ Sudoku

Fill in all the empty cells in the grid so that each row, each column and each 3x3 block contains all the digits from 1-9.

		9	3		4	8		
	7		5		1		6	
	6						3	
5	4			8			2	3
			1	4	3			
3	9			2			8	1
	5						1	
	8		6		9		4	
		7	4		8	6		

BRAINSTRETCHER

Choose the lettered answer that best copies the pattern of the first link. Some lateral thinking is required.

Leo is to *Virgo*, as *Aquarius* is to:

(a) Pisces (b) Aries (c) Gemini (d) Capricorn

★ **123**

Fill each blank square in the grid with the number 1, 2 or 3 so that each completed row and column has an equal number of 1s, 2s and 3s. Each bold rectangular block must contain all three numbers, and no two horizontally or vertically adjacent squares may contain the same number.

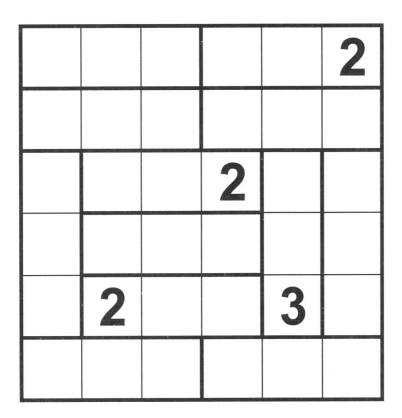

SUDOKU SUM

Write a digit from 0-9 in each of the five blank spaces to make a calculation that works. No digit may be repeated in the sum.

```
    2  _  _
+   _  3  9
_____
    6  _  _
```

★★ Codeword

Can you crack the code and complete the grid? Each letter of the alphabet appears at least once in the grid, and is represented by the same number throughout. The letters we've decoded should help you to identify other letters and words in the grid.

8		13		18		18	8	8		23		22		3
3	13	24	14	14	22	25		3	13	24	3	23	9	16
15		4		12		25		18		15		9		26
24	4	26	18	24	15		17	15	7	23	23	7	2	24
23				22		22				11				20
3	22	4	26	3	22	25		7	15	24	19	18	4	24
		18		16		24		15		3		21		22
5 J	24	14	12		8	3	24	14	1		20	22	14	25
18 A		14		25		7		18		21		15		
17 B	15	18	6	24	22	15		3	13	24	8	3	22	15
17				8				22		14				22
22	8	23	7	15	3	22	25		18	3	15	24	11	4
15		15		7		16		18		18		8		22
22	10	11	18	17	2	22		19	24	19	19	2	22	25
25		12		22		25	11	22		22		22		16

A̶ B̶ C D E F G H I I̶ K L M N O P Q R S T U V W X Y Z

1	2	3	4	5 J	6	7	8	9	10	11	12	13
14	15	16	17 B	18 A	19	20	21	22	23	24	25	26

★ One-Way Streets

The diagram represents a pattern of streets. A and B are parking spaces, and the black squares are shops. Find the route that starts at A, passes through all the shops exactly once, and ends at B. Arrows indicate one-way traffic for that block only. No block or intersection may be entered more than once.

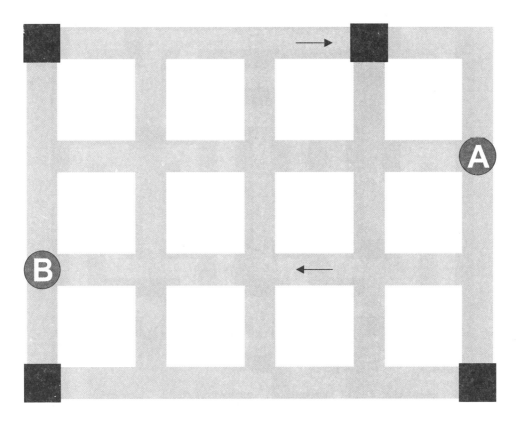

TAKE TWO

Take two consecutive letters from each of the three words, in order, to spell a six-letter word.

Example: <u>TR</u>AP M<u>IN</u>D FR<u>OM</u>
Answer: RANDOM

DRIP AGED BONY

★ Sequence Maze

Enter the maze at the bottom left corner, pass through all the coloured squares exactly once, then exit at the bottom right corner, all without retracing your path. You may not pass through two squares of the same colour consecutively.

MAKE TRACKS

Lay the 'sleepers' of the track by writing the answers to the clues in the numbered Down spaces. Then work out the two 'rail' answers, reading across. The 'rail' answers, which are not necessarily single words, are types of financial trader.

1 Organ used to eat and speak
2 Absence of war
3 Geographical sphere
4 Register
5 Dissuade

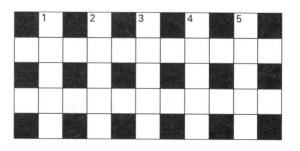

★ Star Search

Find the stars that are hidden in some of the blank squares. The numbered squares indicate how many stars are hidden in the squares adjacent to them (including diagonally). There is never more than one star in any square.

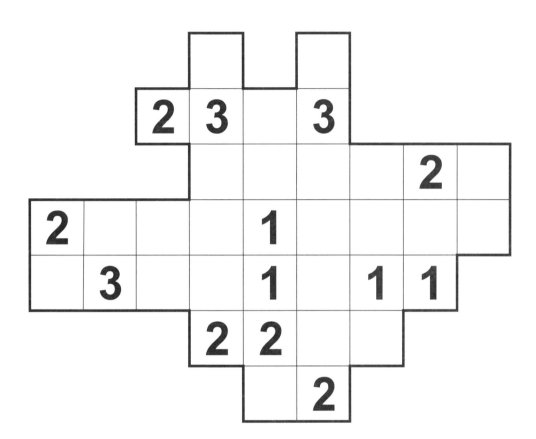

TELEPHONE TRIOS

Using the numbers and letters on the telephone keypad, what three seven-letter words, names or phrases on a common theme can be formed from the numbers below?

2768437 __ __ __ __ __ __ __

4726372 __ __ __ __ __ __ __

4872263 __ __ __ __ __ __ __

1	ABC 2	DEF 3
GHI 4	JKL 5	MNO 6
PRS 7	TUV 8	WXY 9
*	0	#

★★ Pieceword

Fit the blocks together in the empty grid to complete the crossword. Answers to the Across clues fit somewhere in the row with that number. The grid pattern follows biaxial symmetry, that is, the left corresponds to the right, and the top to the bottom.

BIAXIAL SYMMETRY PATTERN

ACROSS

1 Scrape mark on a shoe • Lethal

2 Wild marjoram

3 Person who sells bread • Full of holes

4 Regarded smugly

5 Arouse • Go in

6 Made small waves

7 Hue, shade • Reared

8 Fanatical

9 Bracken • Amusement, pastime

10 Breathe new life into

11 Soothing ointment • Performed on stage

12 Captivated

13 Join as one • Restaurant guest

14 Breathing passage

15 Number of notes in an octave • Terminated

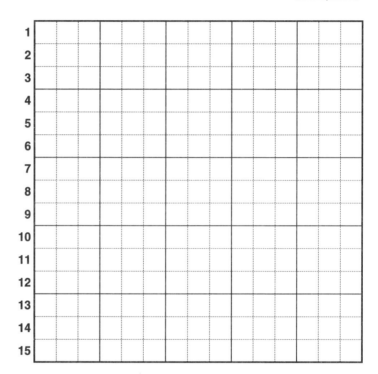

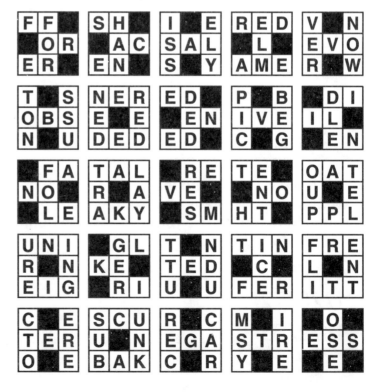

★ Wordsearch – Islands

Find the 23 listed islands that are hidden in the grid. They may read horizontally, vertically or diagonally, and either backwards or forwards.

Baffin
Borneo
Celebes
Cuba
Cyprus
Greenland
Hispaniola
Hokkaido
Honshu
Iceland
Ireland
Java
Luzon
Madagascar
Malta
Mindanao
New Guinea
Sakhalin
Sri Lanka
Sulawesi
Sumatra
Tasmania
Victoria

```
J G A S H O H T A S M A N I A
T A A B I U C O G O E N R O B
M Q V I S Y D R K N I F F A B
G U R A P N E C K K I Z F N X
D U W R A E S A K H A L I N S
P M U L N H P I C R J I W F U
I S E L I R A C S A G A D A M
M C A S O O E V E E B N A O A
I N L E L A N D I T W T T K T
D V V B A N I U N C L A N Q R
K A X E C A U H H A T A L F A
Z W C L U D G S M S L O O U Q
S B X E B N W J V I N E R E S
O Y D C A I E Z R R L O R I Y
L U Z O N M N S K D L J H I A
```

CHOP AND CHANGE

Delete one letter from the word ANTIQUES and rearrange the rest to get a judicial process.

Brain Breather

Cash Cows

What have cows and money got in common, you might ask? Quite a lot, linguistically speaking. The original meaning of the word *cattle* was personal property or wealth. Under a feudal system, where ordinary people could only lease land from their king or lord, not purchase it, wealth was measured in livestock. A related word is *chattel*, which also originally meant property or money. Both of these words are etymologically linked to *capital*, from the Latin word for head, but which also has the meaning 'a principal sum of money'.

Despite Britain having been part of the Roman Empire until AD 410, Latin words like capital only entered the English language in great numbers after the Norman Conquest of 1066. The Anglo-Saxons, who spoke Old English, generally wrote inscriptions not in Latin but in a Runic alphabet. The Runic alphabet, also known as the *futhorc*, developed and changed over the centuries but in the early stages it consisted of 26 characters, or runes, the first of which was *feoh*. Like cattle and chattel, the word *feoh* denoted both cattle and wealth. *Feoh* is the origin of the word *fee* – in Old English a *fee-house* was both a treasury and a cattle-shed.

English words beginning *pecu* often have meanings related to money – pecuniary, for instance. Peculiar was once a noun with the meaning 'an individual's personal property' and a peculator meant an embezzler. These words are derived from the Latin *pecus*, which means – yes, you guessed it – cattle or herd of livestock.

They may not look it, but the Latin word *pecus* and the Old English word *feoh* are cognates, which means they are descended from a common ancestor. The 19th-century German linguist Jacob Grimm (one of the storytelling Brothers Grimm) realised that a 'p' sound in ancient, or classical, Indo-European languages – namely Latin, Greek and Sanskrit – became an 'f' sound in the later Germanic languages. Thus in English (a Germanic language) we say *father* and in German it is *Vater* (v is pronounced f in German), while the Latin, Greek and Sanskrit equivalents are *pater*, *pateras* and *pita* respectively. Similarly, in accordance with Grimm's Law, *pedem* (Latin), *poda* (Greek) and *padam* (Sanskrit) became *foot* and *Fuss* in English and German.

Wealth is no longer measured by how many cows we own, but we still find bovine terms and money linked in common expressions. A *cash cow* is a marketing term for an unusually good moneymaking product or venture, and a *bull market* on the stock exchange means that share prices are rising.

★★ Line Drawing

Draw two straight lines, each from one edge of the square to another edge, to create four regions, each one containing four numbers that add up to an even number.

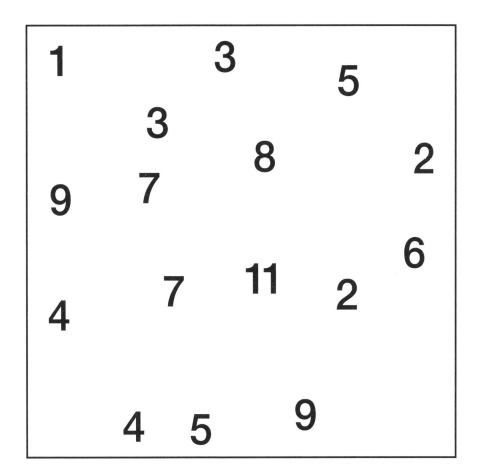

THREE OF A KIND

Find three hidden words in the sentence that, read in order, go together in some way.

Example: Re**st and** p**lan day** outsi**de liver**pool
Answer: **STAND AND DELIVER**

Cover these tomato plants with a net

★ ABC

Enter the letters A, B and C into the diagram so that each row and column has exactly one A, one B and one C, leaving one blank box in each row and column. The letters outside the diagram indicate the first letter encountered, moving in the direction of the arrow.

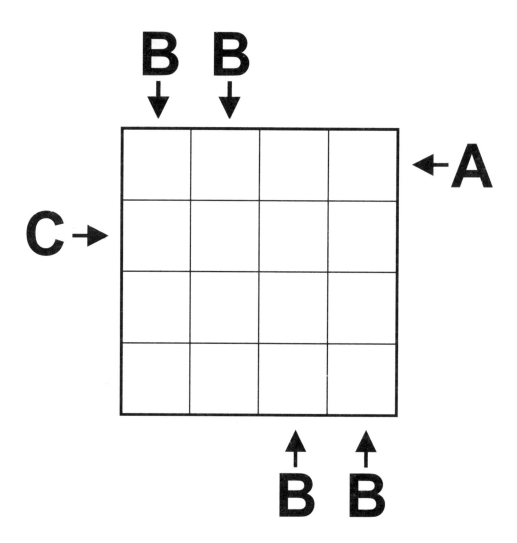

BRAINSTRETCHER

Choose the lettered answer that best copies the pattern of the first link. Some lateral thinking is required.

3 is to *degrees*, as *4* is to:

(a) sides   (b) centimetres   (c) angles   (d) tops

★★ Jig-a-Link

With the help of the starter word, fit all the listed words into the grid.

3 letters
Bus
Dab
Ill
Lie
Owe
Pad
Phi
Rye

4 letters
Asti
Axed
Blip
Dado
Dram
Ever
Grog
Into
Nero
Pull
Rota
Sump
Tang
Tire
Tows
Urdu

5 letters
~~Anode~~
Aside
Debar
Easel
Eerie
Egret
House
Mourn
Nymph
Oxbow
Quail
Reuse
Rosti
Smart
Stamp
Twist

6 letters
Battle
Lodged
Loomed
Mishap
Musing
Pantry
Superb
Unplug

7 letters
Blender
Farming
Flooded
Heeding
Laundry
Nuptial
Prodigy
Renewal
Residue
Risotto
Rostrum
Turkish

9 letters
Deciduous
Embroider
Manhandle
Rehydrate
Reticence
Watchable

★★ What a Pane

Which two of the glass fragments should be used to repair the church window?

BETWEENER

What three-letter word can be inserted between the two words below to make a well-known expression with each?

DRY __ __ __ WILD

★ Wordsearch – Collective Nouns

Find the 25 listed words, all collective nouns, that are hidden in the grid. They may read horizontally, vertically or diagonally, and either backwards or forwards. The animals to which the terms refer are listed with the grid answer. Collective nouns are also featured in the Brain Breather – Group Discussions – on page 82.

Bevy
Brood
Business
Charm
Clowder
Covey
Crash
Desert
Exaltation
Flock
Gaggle
Herd
Knot
Murder
Murmuration
Pack
Parliament
Pride
Rabble

K	W	Y	F	S	F	E	G	V	N	P	R	V	K	T
C	C	G	C	H	Q	L	O	S	O	A	M	R	U	B
R	L	A	X	R	D	B	G	N	I	R	P	S	E	Q
A	S	O	P	E	A	B	T	I	T	L	H	V	E	M
S	X	S	W	W	E	A	V	D	A	I	Y	E	U	P
H	L	Q	E	D	Z	R	U	B	R	A	H	R	R	W
B	U	S	I	N	E	S	S	J	U	M	D	A	K	D
B	L	R	Y	E	D	R	T	W	M	E	R	C	J	R
B	P	S	E	S	G	N	W	E	R	N	H	A	T	K
O	Z	B	V	S	D	I	I	X	U	T	S	R	H	E
S	C	H	O	O	L	F	W	K	M	T	E	O	L	C
P	T	M	C	J	C	A	E	Z	N	S	R	G	J	N
N	O	I	T	A	T	L	A	X	E	U	G	O	N	M
Y	N	I	K	C	O	L	F	D	A	A	S	N	O	G
Y	K	L	H	B	R	O	O	D	G	Y	U	P	H	P

School
Shrewdness

Spring
Troop

Unkindness
Watch

INITIAL REACTION

The words of a well-known proverb or saying have been reduced to their initial letters. Can you restore the missing words?

B L T N _____

★ Find the Ships

Determine the position of the 10 ships listed on the right of the grid. The ships may be oriented either horizontally or vertically. A square with wavy lines indicates water and will not contain part of a ship. The numbers at the edge of the grid indicate how many squares in that row or column contain parts of ships. When all 10 ships are correctly placed in the grid, no two of them will touch each other, not even diagonally. You'll find tips for solving this puzzle in our masterclass on pages 4-5.

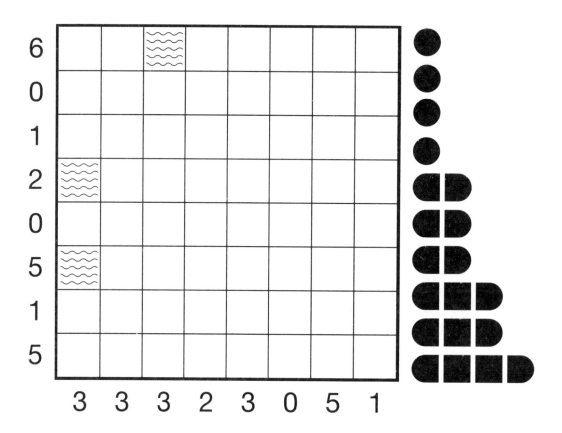

ALTER EGO

Solve the anagram contained in the bold capital letters of the clue to find the name of a celebrity. Do you know their real name?

LAUGH, HONK and grapple this man

_____

★★ Sudoku

Fill in all the empty cells in the grid so that each row, each column and each 3x3 block contains all the digits from 1-9.

4	6	7					9	5
			6			4		
		5	3				7	
	2		4					9
9		8		5		1		7
6					7		2	
	1				9	7		
		9			2			
5	4					9	6	8

LOGICAL

See if you can solve this mini logic problem in your head before writing anything down.

Ginger, Tabby and Fluffy won the top three places at a national cat show. The silver medal went to Tabby, who was not from London. Ginger from Glasgow finished behind the cat from Liverpool. Where was Fluffy from and where did he finish?

★★ Crossword

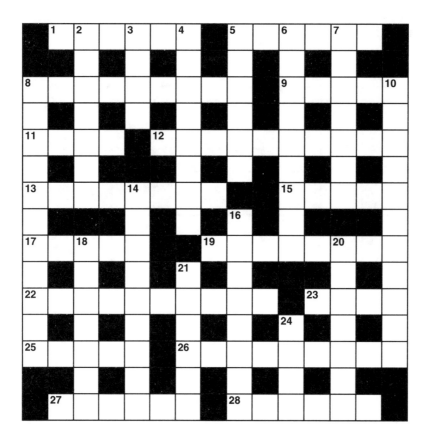

ACROSS

1 Source of gum arabic (6)
5 Mariner, sailor (6)
8 Boundless (9)
9 Completely flooded (5)
11 Melodies, tunes (4)
12 Torvill and Dean's sport (3-7)
13 Spacious layout with few barriers (4-4)
15 Act of stealing (5)
17 Postpone (5)
19 Cyd ___, *Silk Stockings* star (8)
22 With nothing below (10)
23 Bond villain played by Richard Kiel (4)
25 ___ Marbles, Parthenon sculptures (5)
26 Wear informal clothes (5,4)
27 Wreckage (6)
28 Thinly scattered (6)

DOWN

2 Unit of food energy value (7)
3 Arrived, turned up (4)
4 Dictator (8)
5 Gratuitous cruelty (6)
6 Fine-grained translucent gypsum (9)
7 Greed (7)
8 Inevitable (11)
10 Crime of being a traitor to one's own country (4,7)
14 Co-possessor (4-5)
16 Rumours (8)
18 Exhaustion (7)
20 Cliff Richard's old backing group (7)
21 Avoids, shirks (6)
24 Earth's largest continent (4)

★ Fences

Connect adjacent dots with vertical or horizontal lines, so that a single loop with no crossings or branches is formed in the grid. Each number indicates how many lines surround it. Square spaces with no number may be surrounded by any number of lines.

```
2   2     0   3
3 3 2     2   1
2             1

          2 3

      0 3

3                 2
3   0       0 2 2
3   2       3   3
```

ADDITION SWITCH

Switch the positions of two of the digits in this incorrect sum to make a calculation that works.

$$
\begin{array}{r}
5\,0\,1 \\
+\,9\,3\,8 \\
\hline
6\,4\,7
\end{array}
$$

★★ Split Decisions

In this crossword without clues, each answer consists of two words that share common letters, but diverge into different words through the consecutive letters given. All answers are common words; no proper nouns (names), phrases or hyphenated words are used. More than one word pair may fit a particular section of the grid, but only one of the pairs will correctly link up with all the other word pairs.

CHOP AND CHANGE

Delete one letter from the word **PINNACLE** and rearrange the rest to get a type of bird.

★  **123**

Fill each blank square in the grid with the number 1, 2 or 3 so that each completed row and column has an equal number of 1s, 2s and 3s. Each bold rectangular block must contain all three numbers, and no two horizontally or vertically adjacent squares may contain the same number.

		3			
					2
3			**2**		
	1				**1**

SUDOKU SUM

Write a digit from 0-9 in each of the five blank spaces to make a calculation that works. No digit may be repeated in the sum.

```
    3  1  _
+   _  _  9
-----------
    _  6  _
```

★★ Skeleton Crossword

Using the clue numbers and black squares already in the grid to get you started, fill in the black squares as well as the answers to complete this crossword. The grid pattern follows biaxial symmetry, that is, the left corresponds to the right, and the top to the bottom.

ACROSS

1 Make louder
5 Spouse of a reigning monarch
9 Self-satisfied
12 Barren, dry
14 View narrowing towards the horizon
15 Use your tongue to drink
16 Ben ___, highest mountain in the British Isles
18 Pretence
20 Plunge
21 Painting, generally
22 Step of a ladder
23 Fringe benefit
24 Horoscope lion
27 Organ of sight
28 Place for posting bulletins
29 Aggressively male
32 *Catcher in the ___*, novel by JD Salinger
33 Fertile desert spot
36 Exclusively
38 Longish story
40 Study of animal life
41 Seek advice from

DOWN

2 The Three Wise Men from the East
3 Heel over, as a ship
4 Viral infection
6 Rowing blade
7 Flank
8 Flat round Indian bread
10 Fault, defect
11 Sugar-coated
12 Outrage
13 Furnace for burning waste
14 Pointless destruction
17 Fusion
18 Kitchen garment
19 Unclothed
25 Spine-chilling
26 Monastic building
30 High-pitched saxophone
31 Cry of a wolf
34 Crawling insects
35 Hero, object of worship
37 Ship's journal
39 Past, gone

★ Hitori

Black out certain squares in the grid so that no digit appears more than once in any row or column. Blacked-out squares may not touch each other horizontally or vertically, and all remaining squares must form a single continuous area.

4	5	1	2	2
2	2	2	5	4
2	4	3	4	5
3	3	3	4	1
3	1	5	2	1

OPPOSITE ATTRACTION

Unscramble the letters in the phrase COW MOLAR to form two common words that are opposites of each other.

Example: MILL BAGS
Answer: BIG and SMALL

_____   _____

★★ Missing Links

Find the three pentagons that are linked together, but linked to no other pentagons in the diagram.

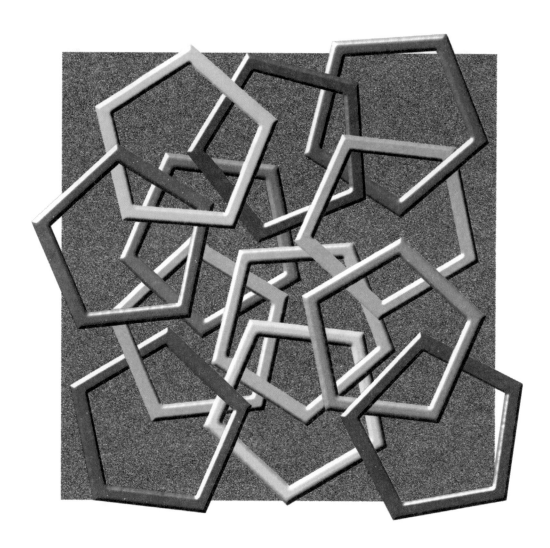

TAKE TWO

Take two consecutive letters from each of the three words, in order, to spell a six-letter word.

CAST COPE TACT

★★★ Killer Sudoku

As in regular sudoku, fill all the empty cells in the grid so that each row, each column and each 3x3 block contains all the digits from 1-9. In addition, the digits in each dotted-line shape must add up to the number given in the top left corner of the shape, and no digit may be repeated within each dotted shape.

15	3	12		14		7		10
		18			8		17	
	14		10	20		12		5
8							11	
16		7		10				17
14	11	15	3	11	6	4		
						12		12
6	4		17		15			
	14		10		14		3	

BRAINSTRETCHER

Choose the lettered answer that best copies the pattern of the first link. Some lateral thinking is required.

Indonesia is to *one*, as *Liechtenstein* is to:
(a) two (b) eight (c) ten (d) fifty

★★★ Dateline

Write the numerical answers to the clues in the grid and you'll discover a date in the shaded squares. Which dictator's rule formally ended on this date?

ACROSS

1 Multiply *45 Down* by months in four years
5 30% of *21 Down*
9 Average of *1 Across*, *48 Across* and *23 Down*
11 Treble *43 Across*
12 Divide *14 Across* by 13
13 Sides on ten octagons
14 Treble *27 Down*
15 Eleven pairs
17 Add days in February 2010 to *45 Down*
19 105% of *13 Across*
20 Rearrange *47 Across*
24 Subtract *15 Across* from *27 Down*
26 Multiply *5 Across* by *11 Across*
30 Subtract years in a decade from *19 Across*
31 Divide *6 Down* by *41 Across*
32 Two-thirds of *26 Across*
33 Subtract degrees in a right-angle from *24 Across*
35 Add *10 Down* to *22 Down*
38 Eight-sevenths of *19 Across*
39 Add 150% of *15 Across* to *43 Across*
41 Total days in July and August
42 Add three-quarters of a century to *28 Down*
43 Square the second digit of *5 Across*
44 Add one-quarter of *19 Across* to *15 Across*
46 14 Across plus *24 Across* less *13 Across*
47 One-third of *34 Down* plus 1,160
48 Multiply *40 Down* by the digit total of *24 Across*
49 150% of *21 Down*

DOWN

2 Add *17 Across* to *48 Across*
3 Double *44 Across*, then subtract from *43 Down*
4 Roman numerals MMCCXIV
5 Add *3 Down* to *8 Down*

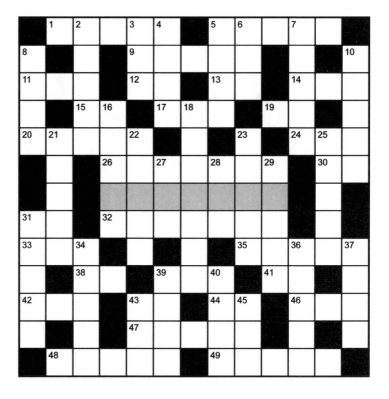

6 Two-thirds of 1,395
7 Divide *18 Down* by 21
8 Subtract *43 Across* from *37 Down*
10 Multiply *46 Across* by 17
16 Subtract *42 Across* from *23 Down*
18 Next in series 843,660 902,927 962,194…
21 Multiply minutes in half-an-hour by 2,205
22 Subtract *39 Across* from *7 Down*
23 200% of *31 Down*
25 Subtract 2,628 from one-hundred thousand
27 Subtract *15 Across* from *11 Across*
28 Double *24 Across*
29 Treble *1 Across*
31 Reverse *48 Across*
34 Add 450% of *15 Across* to *49 Across*
36 Quadruple 4,133 then subtract from *34 Down*
37 Divide *5 Across* by *31 Across*
39 Days in 163 weeks
40 Multiply *33 Across* by 41
43 Add hours in a day to *39 Across*, then reverse
45 Subtract *19 Across* from *42 Across*

★★ One-Way Streets

The diagram represents a pattern of streets. A and B are parking spaces, and the black square is a shop. Find the route that starts at A, passes through the shop, and ends at B. Arrows indicate one-way traffic for that block only. No block or intersection may be entered more than once.

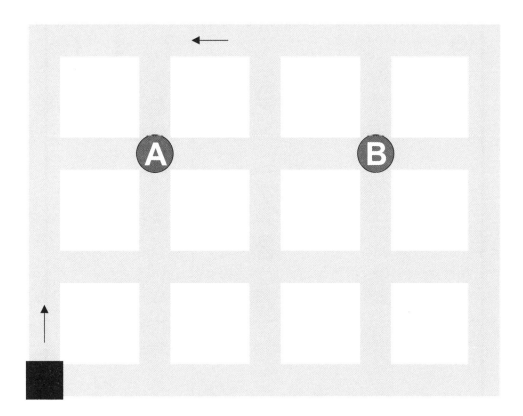

MAKE TRACKS

Lay the 'sleepers' of the track by writing the answers to the clues in the numbered Down spaces. Then work out the two 'rail' answers, reading across. The 'rail' answers, which are not necessarily single words, are people who engage in hazardous activities.

1   Japanese sofa bed
2   Exact copy
3   Indian musical instrument
4   Recite repeatedly
5   Soft flat hat

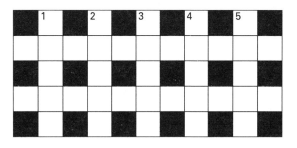

★ Hyper-Sudoku

Fill in the empty cells so that every row, column, 3x3 block and each of the four 3x3 grey regions contains all of the digits from 1-9.

9		2				7	4	6
	7			9	4	5		3
	3	8		7	9	1		
8		4	1	7	3		6	
	6			2	9			1
2			5				9	
	4				2			
		9	1	8				
		9						8

INITIAL REACTION

Some words of a well-known proverb or saying have been reduced to their initial letters. Can you restore the missing words?

A F and H M A S P _____

★ Star Search

Find the stars that are hidden in some of the blank squares. The numbered squares indicate how many stars are hidden in the squares adjacent to them (including diagonally). There is never more than one star in any square.

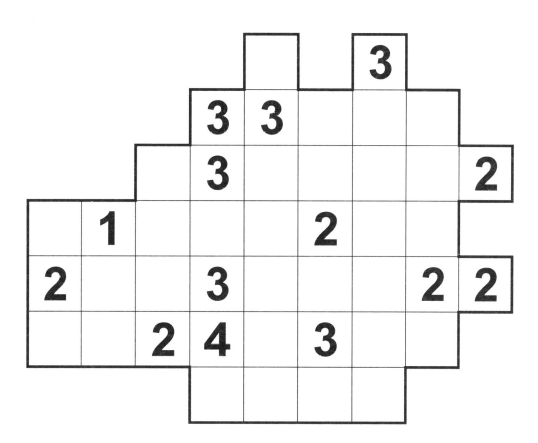

TELEPHONE TRIOS

Using the numbers and letters on the telephone keypad, what three seven-letter words, names or phrases on a common theme can be formed from the numbers below?

2773273   __ __ __ __ __ __ __

2663678   __ __ __ __ __ __ __

2667653   __ __ __ __ __ __ __

1	ABC 2	DEF 3
GHI 4	JKL 5	MNO 6
PRS 7	TUV 8	WXY 9
✱	0	#

★★ Codeword

Can you crack the code and complete the grid? Each letter of the alphabet appears at least once in the grid, and is represented by the same number throughout. The letters we've decoded should help you to identify other letters and words in the grid.

25	21	26	20	1	21		17	20	23	5	19	21	1	1
5		13		15		21		2		19		8		21
1	10	9	16	21	1	12	20	19		14	18	2	11	21
11		9		20		26		14		21		25		21
2	19	25	21	18	1	21	20		3	18	21	21	4	21
1		1				13		20		24				25
	1	15	20	11	16	13	21	25		21	20	1	21	25
14		9		9		5		25		11		20		7
9	3	14	21	19		1	11	18	2	14	5	19	7	
3				1		15		21				11		20
2	19	5	22	2	21		20	1	26	21	1	14	9	1
		19		12		10		1		18		2		11
11	20	11	14	5		5	19	21	26	18	5	20	14	21
20		2		19		13		25		9		18		19
12	20	18	5	6	9	13	25		10	18	21	7	21	25

A B C D E F G H I J K L M̷ N O P Q R S̷ T U̷ V W X Y Z

1 S	2 U	3	4	5	6	7	8	9	10	11	12 M	13
14	15	16	17	18	19	20	21	22	23	24	25	26

★ ABC

Enter the letters A, B and C into the diagram so that each row and column has exactly one A, one B and one C, leaving one blank box in each row and column. The letters outside the diagram indicate the first letter encountered, moving in the direction of the arrow.

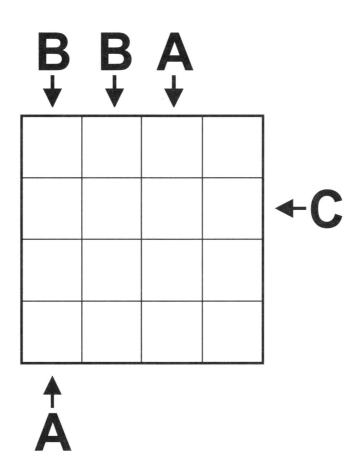

CLUELESS CROSSWORD

Complete the crossword with common seven-letter words, not using names (proper nouns), based entirely on the letters already filled in for you.

★★★ Skeleton Crossword

Using the clue numbers and black squares already in the grid to get you started, fill in the black squares as well as the answers to complete this crossword. The grid follows a fully symmetrical pattern.

ACROSS

1 Grasp, hug

5 Punctual

10 Egg-shaped

11 ___ Marvin, *The Dirty Dozen* actor

12 Melodies

13 Welsh national vegetable

14 Snake also known as the viper

15 Partially burn

18 Salacious

20 Ignore orders

22 First month of the year

24 Largest lake in central Europe

26 Prized sea fish

28 Narrow rainwater channel

29 Potato

33 Span of geological time

34 Idol, deity

35 HG ___, *The Time Machine* author

36 Shellfish delicacy

37 Mount for a moving crane

DOWN

2 Letting contract

3 Scottish turnip

4 Vacation

5 Act the part

6 Ingredient of porridge

7 Suffolk ___, draught horse

8 Item worn by a dog

9 Off course

16 Morsel

17 Sacred song

19 Large vase

21 Small flying mammal

22 Talk rapidly

23 Less advanced in years

24 Canine symbol of Britain

25 Naked sun-worshipper

27 Narrative

30 Relating to the Arctic or Antarctic

31 Seventh Sunday after Easter

32 Large aquatic bird

★★ Sudoku

Fill in all the empty cells in the grid so that each row, each column and each 3x3 block contains all the digits from 1-9.

		3		6		9		
	9		1		4			
8						2		7
	3				8		9	
7				5				2
	4		9				7	
6		5						4
		8		5		3		
		8		2		7		

AND SO ON

Unscramble the letters in the phrase BREATHY GIRL to form two words that are linked by the word 'and' in a common phrase.

_____ and _____

★★ Crossword

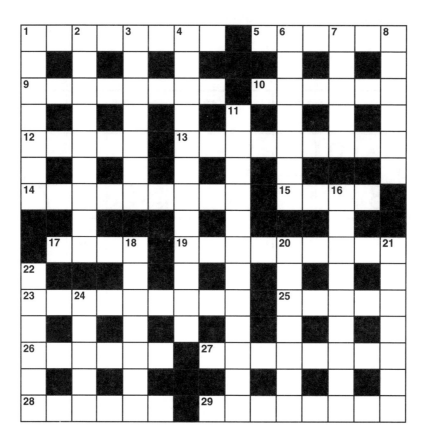

ACROSS

1 Excessive force, brutality (8)

5 Frozen spike of water (6)

9 Suggestive (of) (8)

10 Distilled liquor (6)

12 Opening passage of music (5)

13 Capital punishment (9)

14 Approach of darkness (9)

15 Every (4)

17 Family chart (4)

19 Lowest musical voice in women (9)

23 Grasp the meaning of (5,2,2)

25 Sedated (5)

26 Lisa Kudrow's character in *Friends* (6)

27 Creature that eats anything (8)

28 Signify, mean (6)

29 Follower (8)

DOWN

1 Account (7)

2 Veteran (3,6)

3 ___ Gould, *M*A*S*H* actor (7)

4 Legal process of selling property (12)

6 Large pill (7)

7 Queen's favourite breed of dog (5)

8 Lengthen, prolong (6)

11 Knowledgeable (4,8)

16 American mobile? (9)

18 Display (7)

20 Alcoholic drink of a burgundy colour (3,4)

21 Fabric offcut (7)

22 Inclined (6)

24 Spike on a plant (5)

★★ Line Drawing

Draw three straight lines, each from one edge of the square to another edge, to create four regions, each one containing three words that have something in common.

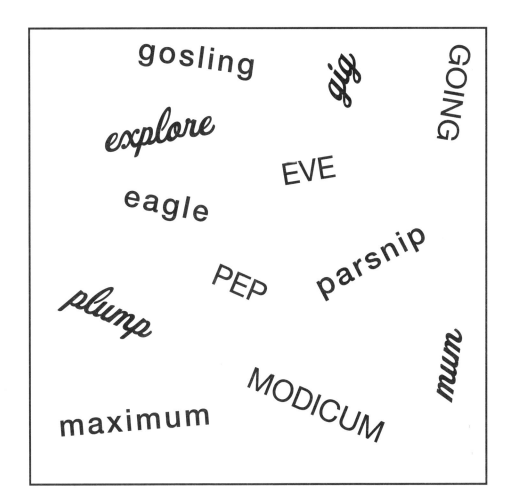

BETWEENER

What five-letter word can be inserted between the two words below to make a well-known expression with each?

NEW __ __ __ __ __ HANDLE

★ Find the Ships

Determine the position of the 10 ships listed on the right of the grid. The ships may be oriented either horizontally or vertically. A square with wavy lines indicates water and will not contain part of a ship. The numbers at the edge of the grid indicate how many squares in that row or column contain parts of ships. When all 10 ships are correctly placed in the grid, no two of them will touch each other, not even diagonally. You'll find tips for solving this puzzle in our masterclass on pages 4-5.

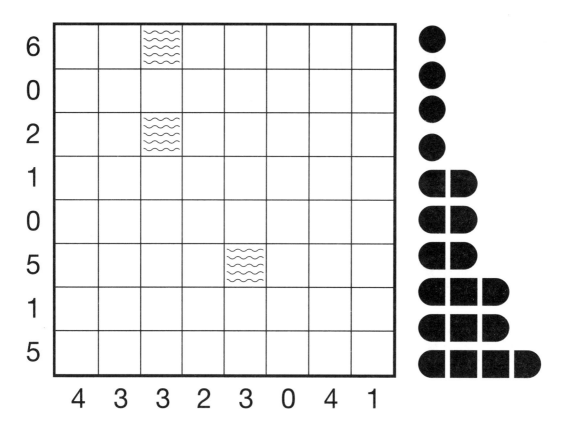

MAKE TRACKS

Lay the 'sleepers' of the track by writing the answers to the clues in the numbered Down spaces. Then work out the two 'rail' answers, reading across. The 'rail' answers, which are not necessarily single words, can be found in a salon.

1 Marine reef growth
2 Bedeck
3 Baby-delivering bird?
4 North American elk
5 Bar for prising

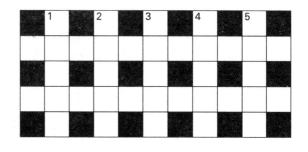

★★ Fences

Connect adjacent dots with vertical or horizontal lines, so that a single loop with no crossings or branches is formed in the grid. Each number indicates how many lines surround it. Square spaces with no number may be surrounded by any number of lines.

```
1           2
      2   3 2 3
  3     3 0 1
  2               3
  3               1
    2 2 1         3
  3 0 1   1
      2           1
```

ADDITION SWITCH

Switch the positions of two of the digits in this incorrect sum to make a calculation that works.

$$
\begin{array}{r}
7\,1\,6 \\
+\,2\,9\,1 \\
\hline
8\,0\,5
\end{array}
$$

★★★ Skeleton Crossword

Using the clue numbers and black squares already in the grid to get you started, fill in the black squares as well as the answers to complete this crossword. The grid follows a fully symmetrical pattern.

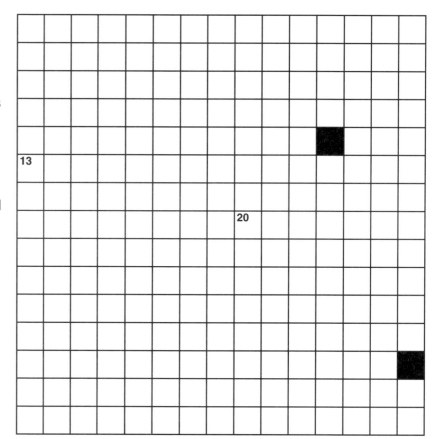

ACROSS

7 Native of Belgrade

8 Freeing from impurities

10 Remain

11 One of the five Great Lakes

12 Tiers

13 Tribe of which Geronimo was a famous chief

15 Gaddafi's nationality

17 Derogatory name for an old woman

19 Capital of Ghana

20 Bicker

22 High-pitched bark

25 Less empty

27 ___ Harry, Blondie singer

28 Throw, toss

30 Italian fashion centre

31 Spanish painter of *The Disasters of War*

32 Narrow, prejudiced

33 Amass

DOWN

1 Nazi secret police

2 Online auction site

3 Old golf club

4 Tapered tube

5 Dr Frankenstein's manservant

6 Wintry character from the Raymond Briggs story

9 Theatrical work

14 ___ Rhodes, British-born South African statesman

16 Advertising text

17 Grass mown and dried for fodder

18 Opening

21 Waiting in line

23 Put into practice

24 Vehicle with handlebars

26 ___ MacDonald, Britain's first Labour prime minister

27 Inventor of the pneumatic tyre

29 Thug, hooligan

31 Stare in wonder

★★ Stamp Collection

Which of the numbered stamps were used to make prints A, B and C?

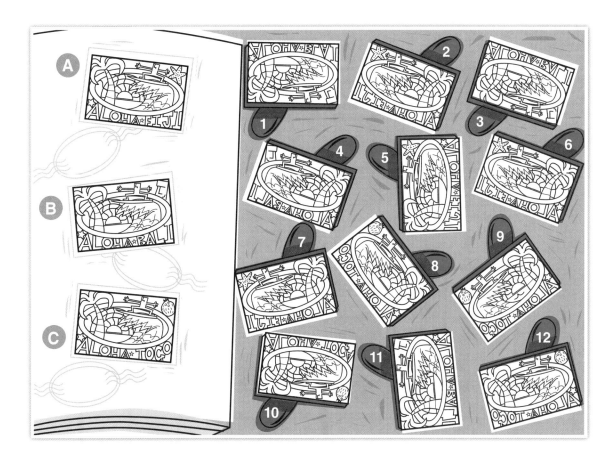

RHYMING TRIO

Rearrange the listed letters to form three one-syllable words that rhyme.

A A E E F H I I R R R

_____   _____   _____

★★ 123

Fill each blank square in the grid with the number 1, 2 or 3 so that each completed row and column has an equal number of 1s, 2s and 3s. Each bold rectangular block must contain all three numbers, and no two horizontally or vertically adjacent squares may contain the same number.

2			2					
							2	
	1			1				
					1			1
			3					
	2					1		
								1
		2						

SUDOKU SUM

Write a digit from 0-9 in each of the five blank spaces to make a calculation that works. No digit may be repeated in the sum.

```
    4 _ 8
+   _ 2 _
  _____
    _ 3 _
```

★ Hitori

Black out certain squares in the grid so that no digit appears more than once in any row or column. Blacked-out squares may not touch each other horizontally or vertically, and all remaining squares must form a single continuous area.

3	4	2	4	1
5	4	5	1	3
1	4	4	3	5
2	3	1	4	4
1	1	1	2	3

OPPOSITE ATTRACTION

Unscramble the letters in the phrase **ELM ROSES** to form two words that are opposites of each other.

_____   _____

★★ Pathfinder – Welsh Place Names

Beginning with WREXHAM (already marked), then moving up, down, left or right (never diagonally), one letter at a time, trace a continuous path in the diagram through the 22 listed towns and cities in Wales.

R	D	W	E	S	T	A	T	H	C	A	S	L
O	A	H	L	I	N	E	T	F	D	R	H	E
F	V	L	L	H	B	N	E	F	I	O	P	W
R	E	Y	Y	P	Y	C	O	P	L	O	N	O
R	R	H	B	R	E	W	N	O	R	E	D	U
O	N	O	R	C	A	Y	T	R	W	X	H	D
G	N	C	E	A	W	S	H	C	A	M	A	N
B	A	A	L	E	A	W	E	N	W	L	L	A
I	E	N	L	S	N	P	O	W	L	T	W	Y
L	L	Y	N	T	R	O	T	S	A	S	Y	T
P	R	T	A	H	K	E	E	P	B	E	R	H
D	E	S	T	O	O	C	H	P	D	G	D	B
A	E	H	Y	L	R	B	M	E	N	E	I	R

Aberystwyth	Llanelli
Bangor	Neath
Brecon	Newport
Bridgend	Pembroke
Caerphilly	Porthcawl
Cardiff	Prestatyn
Chepstow	Rhyl
Conwy	Swansea
Haverfordwest	Tenby
Holyhead	Welshpool
Llandudno	~~Wrexham~~

★★ Dicey Duos

Group the dice into 18 pairs, whose sum may be any number except 7 or 11. The dice in each pair must be connected to each other by a common horizontal or vertical side.

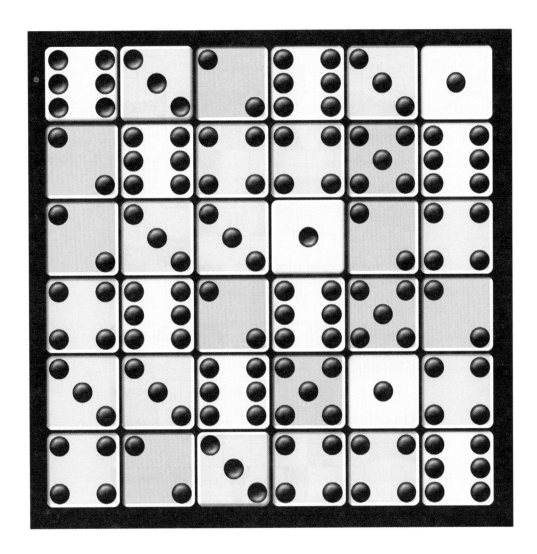

INITIAL REACTION

Some words of a well-known proverb or saying have been reduced to their initial letters. Can you restore the missing words?

O of S O of M _____

★★ Split Decisions

In this crossword without clues, each answer consists of two words that share common letters, but diverge into different words through the consecutive letters given. All answers are common words; no proper nouns (names), phrases or hyphenated words are used. More than one word pair may fit a particular section of the grid, but only one of the pairs will correctly link up with all the other word pairs.

CHOP AND CHANGE

Delete one letter from the word PARCHED and rearrange the rest to get something a member of the clergy would do.

_____

★ Hyper-Sudoku

Fill in the empty cells so that every row, column, 3x3 block and each of the four 3x3 grey regions contains all of the digits from 1-9.

8		7		9		4	6	1
			8	1				7
		1			7	9	8	
	7	6				1		8
			6		9		7	
2	3		7				5	
							3	4
	8	2			4			
		9	5		8	2		6

AND SO ON

Unscramble the letters in the phrase CHASE HECKLE to form two words that are linked by the word 'and' in a common phrase.

——————— and ———————

★★ Codeword

Can you crack the code and complete the grid? Each letter of the alphabet appears at least once in the grid, and is represented by the same number throughout. The letters we've decoded should help you to identify other letters and words in the grid.

	24	11	13	18	■	22	2	5	15	24	■	4	13	17
24	■	4	■	13		13		2	■	6		1	■	13
23	15	1	23	20	2	12		25	6	13	9	2	7	5
4		17	■	7		3		25	■	12		16	■	1
5	4	4	17	■	14	15	16	7		25	15	24	16	10
16	■	5		17		2	■	19		■	24	■		13
■	24	16	10	6	2	24	8	■	20	7	7	23	7	5
16	■	7	■	13		8		15	■	26		2	■	19
21	2	5	2	12	25	■	15	12	8	2	12	25	7	■
2	■		4			14		19		16		25	■	21
24	6	2	12	20	■	4	23	7	12	■	1	10	16	8
			I	**N**	**K**									
16	■	12	■	12		24	■	5	■	24		18	■	2
2	12	7	26	13	11	16	■	11	13	12	22	13	24	24
12	■	23	■	11		6		15	■	4	■	11		16
25	15	16	■	20	12	7	6	16		18	2	20	7	■

A B C D E F G H X̶ J X̶ L M X̶ O P Q R S T U V W X Y Z

1	2 **I**	3	4	5	6	7	8	9	10	11	12 **N**	13
14	15	16	17	18	19	20 **K**	21	22	23	24	25	26

★ Wordsearch – Famous Artists

Find the 27 listed artists that are hidden in the grid. They may read horizontally, vertically or diagonally, and either backwards or forwards.

Chagall
Constable
Gainsborough
Gauguin
Giotto
Goya
Hockney
Hogarth
Holbein
Lowry
Magritte
Matisse
Millais
Munch
Picasso
Pollock
Rembrandt
Renoir
Reynolds
Spencer
Stubbs

K	V	N	J	B	H	R	S	I	A	L	L	I	M	L
I	E	I	R	V	O	R	E	N	O	I	R	C	S	L
S	R	E	E	F	C	G	O	M	V	T	O	M	T	A
M	M	B	L	E	K	A	R	C	B	N	Z	G	U	G
R	E	L	T	L	N	I	Q	E	S	R	R	H	B	A
P	E	O	S	I	E	N	A	T	C	E	A	B	B	H
H	R	H	I	D	Y	S	A	N	T	N	Y	N	S	C
W	V	O	H	R	L	B	C	T	A	R	E	T	D	O
G	G	A	W	G	L	O	I	I	K	U	I	P	S	T
U	A	O	N	E	I	R	N	M	A	T	I	S	S	E
W	L	U	D	G	G	O	F	Y	I	Y	A	L	U	P
S	N	F	G	A	O	U	T	A	E	C	O	Q	V	L
T	E	X	M	U	Z	G	N	T	I	R	J	G	D	X
H	C	N	U	M	I	H	H	P	O	L	L	O	C	K
L	O	H	R	A	W	N	H	T	R	A	G	O	H	Y

Titian
Turner
Van Gogh

Vermeer
Warhol
Whistler

BRAINSTRETCHER

Choose the lettered answer that best copies the pattern of the first link. Some lateral thinking is required.

Castilian is to *Catalan*, as *Hindi* is to:

(a) Bengali (b) Calcutta (c) Arabic (d) Persian

Brain Breather

Group Discussions

How many of the collective nouns on page 49 do you recognise? More to the point, when was the last time you used one of them in conversation? Most of us, alas, no longer lead the sort of lives where we are ever called upon to discuss deserts of lapwings or knots of toads. And though we may remember to say a gaggle of geese, rather than a flock, who among us reserves the term for a group of geese on the ground, while correctly using skein to refer to geese that are airborne?

Special terms describing groups of animals have a long history – towards the end of the 14th century, Chaucer referred to a parliament of birds in his *Canterbury Tales*. Many can be traced to a popular book on hunting and falconry, called *The Book of St Albans*, which was published in the 15th century. This became an indispensable addition to every gentleman's library as upper-class young men took pains to learn the correct terms for animals, as this knowledge set them apart from common-or-garden yeomen. They were known then as terms of *venery*, venery being an old word for hunting and for the animals that were hunted. Since then, so many collective terms have been coined that it is hard to verify their sources, or to distinguish those with a history of general usage from the more fanciful concoctions.

There is usually a logic behind a collective noun. The term parliament, for example, was coined for birds such as rooks because of their tendency to congregate noisily. In many cases, the significance of a collective term may be lost on modern readers. An unkindness of ravens, for example, referred to the belief that ravens pushed their young out of the nest. A murmuration of starlings evokes the sounds made by the birds, while an exaltation of larks refers to their habit of ascending higher and higher into the sky. The term murder as the collective noun for crows may have been inspired by the crow's raucous cry, or come from the bird's symbolism as a harbinger of death or doom.

Although some collective terms have become quaint and outmoded, others remain firmly a part of our modern language. We may no longer talk of a watch of nightingales or charm of goldfinches, but most children know that it is a pride of lions and a school of whales, that sheep come in flocks and cattle in herds.

Coining collective nouns has remained a popular pastime. The focus of invention today seems to be on groups of people. We have come across a lack of principals, a horde (hoard) of misers, a scoop of journalists and a pack of travel agents. And what about a solution of puzzlers?

★★ One-Way Streets

The diagram represents a pattern of streets. P's are parking spaces, and the black squares are shops. Find the route that starts at a parking space, passes through all the shops exactly once, and ends at the other parking space. Arrows indicate one-way traffic for that block only. No block or intersection may be entered more than once.

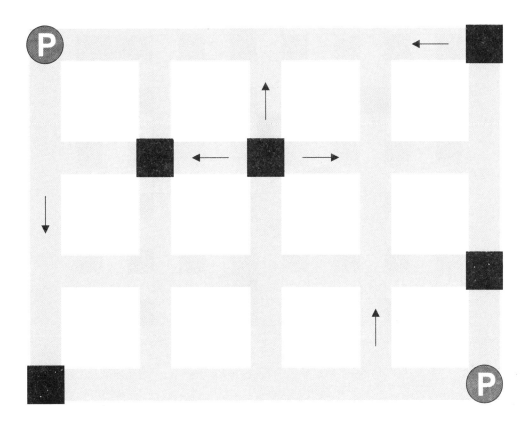

ALTER EGO

Solve the anagram contained in the bold capital letters of the clue to find the name of a celebrity. Do you know their real name?

ODE MEMOIR for GI Jane

★★ Crossword

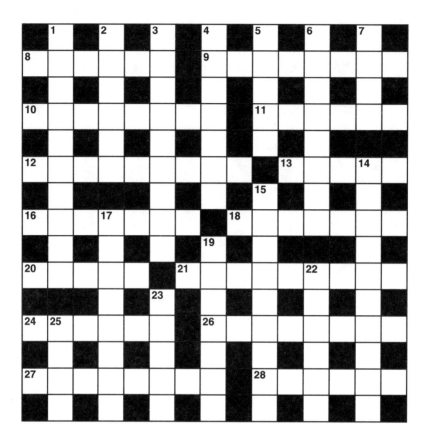

ACROSS

8 Health facility, often devoted to treating specific ailments (6)

9 Universal or broad-minded (8)

10 Regard as perfect (8)

11 Instinctive movement (6)

12 Quickly earned money (1,4,4)

13 Bring about, make happen (5)

16 Food additive code (1-6)

18 Fortunately (7)

20 Decorate, embellish (5)

21 Maximum amount allowed (4,5)

24 Imitator (6)

26 Take a ___, let others do the work (4,4)

27 Suffering the after-effects of alcohol (4-4)

28 Have enough money for (6)

DOWN

1 Unclear (3-7)

2 Chronicles (6)

3 Hastily written (9)

4 High-pitched cry (7)

5 Begin (5)

6 Luggage carrier on the top of a car (4,4)

7 Tell a story without using words (4)

14 Quibble (5,5)

15 Less expensive room in an alehouse (6,3)

17 Wedlock (8)

19 Result of too much tanning (7)

22 Dangerous (6)

23 Heroic (5)

25 Work, especially of music (4)

★★ Pirate Ship Maze

Enter the maze as indicated, pass through all the red dots exactly once, and then exit. You may not retrace your path.

RHYMING TRIO

Rearrange the listed letters to form three one-syllable words that rhyme.

B E E G H I I I R T T T

_____   _____   _____

★★ Star Search

Find the stars that are hidden in some of the blank squares. The numbered squares indicate how many stars are hidden in the squares adjacent to them (including diagonally). There is never more than one star in any square.

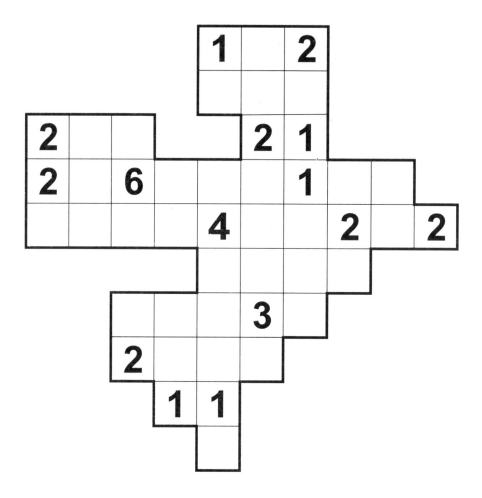

TELEPHONE TRIOS

Using the numbers and letters on the telephone keypad, what three seven-letter words, names or phrases on a common theme can be formed from the numbers below?

	ABC	DEF
1	**2**	**3**
GHI	JKL	MNO
4	**5**	**6**
PRS	TUV	WXY
7	**8**	**9**
*	**0**	**#**

2677422   _ _ _ _ _ _ _

6546292   _ _ _ _ _ _ _

7862872   _ _ _ _ _ _ _

★★ Colour In

This panel for a Tiffany-style table-lamp is to be made in a mosaic of red, blue and green. If no two pieces of the same colour share a border, what colour will the two lettered corner pieces be?

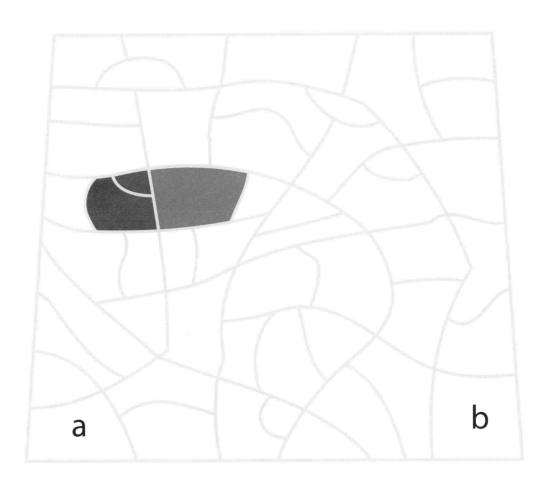

CHOP AND CHANGE

Delete one letter from the word SEVERAL and rearrange the rest to get someone who is on the way out.

★★ Pieceword

Fit the blocks together in the empty grid to complete the crossword. Answers to the Across clues fit somewhere in the row with that number. The grid pattern follows biaxial symmetry, that is, the left corresponds to the right, and the top to the bottom.

BIAXIAL SYMMETRY PATTERN

ACROSS

2 Pelting with rocks • Flow of electricity

4 Bridge arch • Verbose • Aid, often illegally

6 Recess in a church • Adjust your eyes • Thin rope

8 Intensely passionate • Modernise

10 Legend • Emaciated • Friar

12 Affectionate, loving • Flat dish • Cheque counterfoil

14 Male servant • Recording points

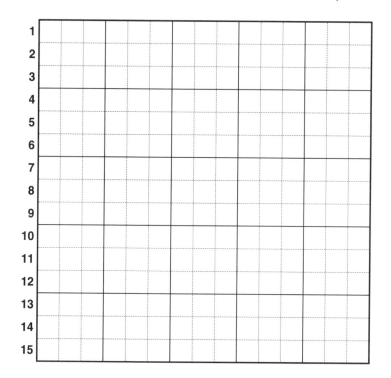

★★ ABC

Enter the letters A, B and C into the diagram so that each row and column has exactly one A, one B and one C, leaving two blank boxes in each row and column. The letters outside the diagram indicate the first letter encountered, moving in the direction of the arrow.

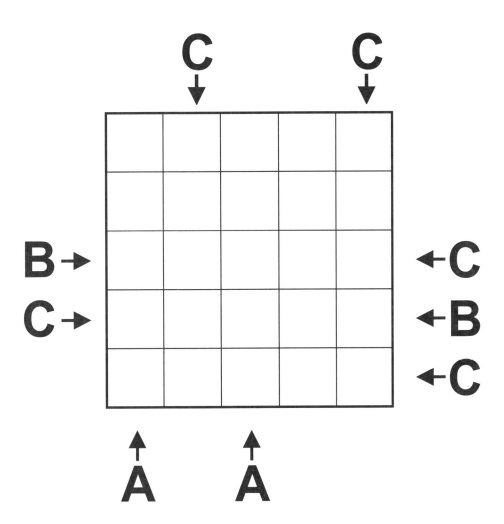

TAKE TWO

Take two consecutive letters from each of the three words, in order, to spell a six-letter word.

YOLK   BEND   PERT

★★ Find the Ships

Determine the position of the 10 ships listed on the right of the grid; one piece has been inserted in the grid to get you started. The ships may be oriented either horizontally or vertically. A square with wavy lines indicates water and will not contain part of a ship. The numbers at the edge of the grid indicate how many squares in that row or column contain parts of ships. When all 10 ships are correctly placed in the grid, no two of them will touch each other, not even diagonally.

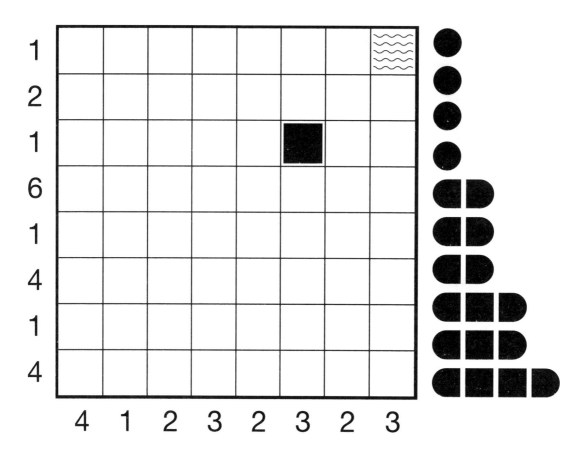

BACK NUMBERS

Starting from the mystery number, calculating each step in turn from left to right will result in the answer given. Work the sum backwards to find that missing first number.

| ? | x 12 | 20% of it | + 25 | double it | + 30 | = 200 |

★★ Pathfinder – Printing Terms

Beginning with BAR CODE (already marked), then moving up, down, left or right (never diagonally), one letter at a time, trace a continuous path in the diagram through the 26 listed words and phrases that are used as printing terms.

```
T  R  Q  Y  T  I  C  E  D  I  D  B  O
O  A  U  S  O  P  A  R  R  N  N  I  I
B  A  B  S  O  B  M  E  O  G  P  O  L
O  R  C  O  D  E  Y  L  B  S  R  F  N
O  K  D  M  A  K  E  I  N  S  E  H  A
L  B  N  E  S  A  L  L  E  L  A  P  R
O  L  E  G  T  G  G  E  A  S  M  I  O
C  K  M  O  H  E  N  Y  R  T  E  N  E
E  D  I  R  B  A  I  N  R  E  R  A  T
O  O  T  E  R  D  R  N  I  K  M  K  R
F  O  R  U  R  G  A  V  S  H  A  G  O
F  F  E  V  A  S  O  W  O  T  N  E  W
S  E  T  V  E  R  W  I  D  A  A  R  T
```

Artwork	Kerning	Raster
~~Bar code~~	Keyline	Varnish
Binding	Laminate	Verso
Book block	Legend	Widow
Border	Magenta	
Bromide	Masthead	
Emboss	Offset	
Folio	Opacity	
Footer	Orphan	
Galley	Press	
Gravure	Quarto	

★★ Drop Zone

The seven columns show stacks of lettered balls – remove a ball and the others above it will drop down in its place. Your task is to remove one ball from each column so that when all the other balls drop down, they spell out six words reading across. What are they, and what word is spelled out by the seven balls you remove?

N	E	T	L	O	R	K
E	T	B	W	N	A	L
P	L	E	R	A	T	E
C	U	I	M	H	O	W
S	O	M	E	I	I	C
T	R	A	F	F	S	N
L	A	N	T	E	R	H

BETWEENER

What five-letter word can be inserted between the two words below to make a well-known expression with each?

VILLAGE __ __ __ __ __ BELT

★★ Sudoku

Fill in all the empty cells in the grid so that each row, each column and each 3x3 block contains all the digits from 1-9.

				3				
	8	4		9	1			
	3		7		8		2	
	5	4				9	7	
1				8				5
	8	9				6	3	
	9		2		1		8	
		1	8		7	4		
				6				

LOGICAL

See if you can solve this mini logic problem in your head before writing anything down.

Emily, Rita and Sue have each chosen to attend a different evening class that takes place on Monday, Tuesday or Wednesday. Rita goes on Tuesday evening, but not to Spanish. Emily does computing, and goes earlier in the week than Sue. If the third class is art, what is Sue studying, and on which evening?

★★★ Killer Sudoku

As in regular sudoku, fill all the empty cells in the grid so that each row, each column and each 3x3 block contains all the digits from 1-9. In addition, the digits in each dotted-line shape must add up to the number given in the top left corner of the shape, and no digit may be repeated within each dotted shape.

ADDITION SWITCH

Switch the positions of two of the digits in this incorrect sum to make a calculation that works.

$$\begin{array}{r} 1\,9\,3 \\ +\,2\,9\,6 \\ \hline 4\,7\,8 \end{array}$$

★★★ Codeword

Can you crack the code and complete the grid? Each letter of the alphabet appears at least once in the grid, and is represented by the same number throughout. The letters we've decoded should help you to identify other letters and words in the grid. If you would like a third starter letter, turn to page 255.

24	13	22	26	13	21	3	4	8		17	21	23	9	9
	11		20		5		18		26		20		20	
1	13	21	23	6	4		17	21	5	14	14	13	8	15
	5		10				20		1		4		4	
16	21	13 (L)	15	10	4	1	1		19	4	10	2	5	21
		13 (A)	4		12		1				16		16	
2	20	10	15	23	5	6		2	13	22	4	10	10	4
	2				21				15				4	
1	2	23	19	19	4	8		2	20	18	19	4	8	4
	23		4				25		19		13			
1	19	13	8	4	15		13	6	6	20	8	10	4	22
	13		11		13		8				7		17	
23	10	25	13	8	18	4	15		1	6	23	17	17	22
	2		15		19		4		20		4		4	
6	22	19	4	15		16	8	13	6	5	6	23	15	4

A̸ B C D E F G H I J K L̸ M N O P Q R S T U V W X Y Z

1	2	3	4	5	6	7	8	9	10	11	12	13 **A**
14	15	16	17	18	19	20	21 **L**	22	23	24	25	26

★★ Hitori

Black out certain squares in the grid so that no digit appears more than once in any row or column. Blacked-out squares may not touch each other horizontally or vertically, and all remaining squares must form a single continuous area.

3	3	2	5	6	2
5	6	4	6	2	2
3	2	4	1	4	6
1	6	5	4	2	6
2	4	6	4	1	5
1	6	3	2	2	1

OPPOSITE ATTRACTION

Unscramble the letters in the phrase **GLIB TITLE** to form two words that are opposites of each other.

_____   _____

★★ Hyper-Sudoku

Fill in the empty cells so that every row, column, 3x3 block and each of the four 3x3 grey regions contains all of the digits from 1-9.

		8				2	4	
						3	8	5
2				6				
	3			7	4	5		
7		3			1			8
5	8	1						
	5			1			2	
			9	8			1	
		6	5					

MAKE TRACKS

Lay the 'sleepers' of the track by writing the answers to the clues in the numbered Down spaces. Then work out the two 'rail' answers, reading across. The 'rail' answers, which are not necessarily single words, are types of shop you might find on the High Street.

1   Unclear, indistinct
2   Entomb
3   _____ fatale, film-noir heroine?
4   Tired, fatigued
5   Precipitous

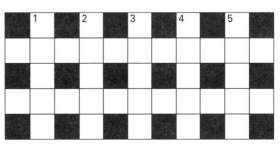

★★★ Crossword

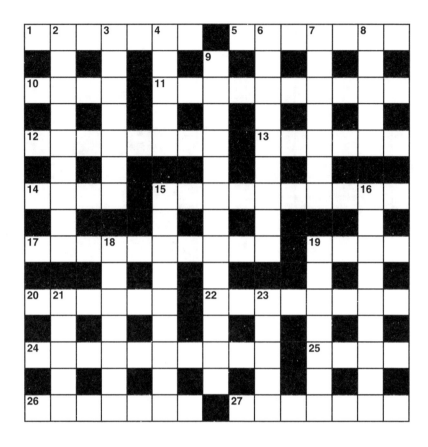

ACROSS

1 Apparition (7)
5 Quarantine (7)
10 Paving stone (4)
11 Female pupil (10)
12 Artist who carves stone (8)
13 In cricket, the bowler's target (6)
14 Corrosive solution (4)
15 Surrender, submit (10)
17 Take in air (4,6)
19 Stare in amazement (4)
20 Peer short-sightedly (6)
22 Workers' interval (3,5)
24 Co-star of Sean Penn and Tim Robbins in *Mystic River* (5,5)

25 Confront (4)
26 Name of Roy Rogers' horse (7)
27 Branch of arithmetic (7)

DOWN

2 Law-enforcement patrol vehicle (6,3)
3 ___ together, patched up (7)
4 Make ready again (5)
6 Timepiece for sporting events (9)
7 Rational (7)
8 Rich layer cake (5)
9 Behaviour that is not entirely honest (5,8)

15 Piece of furniture for indoor games (4,5)
16 Person clicking heel and toe (3,6)
18 Small fish of the cod family (7)
19 Tallest living mammal (7)
21 Peculiar, odd (5)
23 Declare void (5)

★ Wordsearch – Horse Play

The 21 listed names belong to famous horses, both real and fictional. Find the names in the grid, where they may read horizontally, vertically or diagonally, and either backwards or forwards.

Arkle
Black Beauty
Black Bess
Bucephalus
Champion
Cigar
Comanche
Copenhagen
Desert Orchid
Doublet
Incitatus
Marengo
Mr Softee
Nijinsky
Red Rum
Rosinante
Seabiscuit
Shergar
Silver
Topper
Trigger

F	R	T	S	Y	S	B	L	A	C	K	B	E	S	S
F	E	E	U	T	C	U	K	T	X	C	Y	L	H	H
N	D	B	T	U	O	D	L	H	E	V	I	E	X	X
C	R	M	A	A	P	E	W	A	E	L	R	G	O	M
P	U	L	T	E	E	S	T	L	H	G	B	S	A	E
A	M	R	I	B	N	E	K	M	A	P	E	U	E	R
U	S	E	C	K	H	R	C	R	A	A	E	T	O	E
K	S	G	N	C	A	T	Z	H	B	R	F	C	T	D
G	G	G	I	A	G	O	O	I	A	O	E	N	U	U
D	G	I	O	L	E	R	S	D	S	M	A	N	A	B
J	Y	R	N	B	N	C	J	R	P	N	P	I	G	C
E	N	T	Q	R	U	H	M	D	I	R	F	I	Z	O
Q	I	W	N	I	J	I	N	S	K	Y	B	P	O	H
M	U	J	T	V	L	D	O	T	O	P	P	E	R	N
R	E	V	L	I	S	R	E	H	C	N	A	M	O	C

INITIAL REACTION

Some words of a well-known proverb or saying have been reduced to their initial letters. Can you restore the missing words?

I I N U C over S M _____

★★ Go with the Flow

Enter the maze as indicated, pass through all the circles exactly once, then exit. You must go with the flow, making no sharp turns, but may use paths more than once.

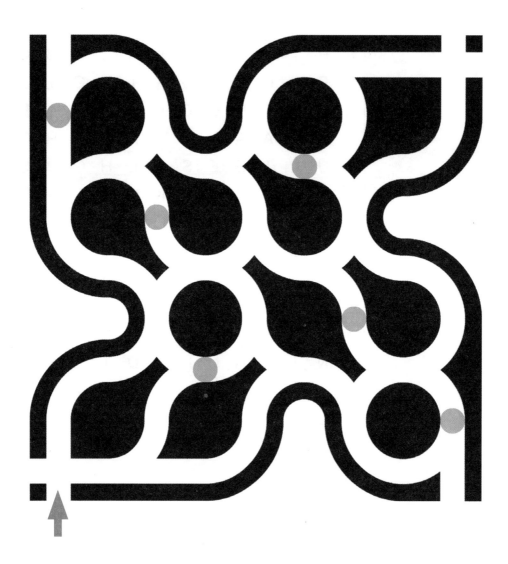

ALTER EGO

Solve the anagram contained in the bold capital letters of the clue to find the name of a celebrity. Do you know their real name?

SENT HIM NEAR to the West Wing

_____

★★ Jig-a-Link

With the help of the starter word, fit all the listed words into the grid.

3 letters
Soy
Way
Yes
Yew

5 letters
Aroma
Bleat
Delhi
Dries
Ghost
Great
Grout
~~Icing~~
Loser
Tulip
Upper
Upset

6 letters
Allege
Annexe
Armour
Asleep
Bikini
Bureau
Enough
Futile
Horrid
Perish
Reboot
Rising
Rubble
Sitcom
Slouch
Uneven

7 letters
Aerobic
Alfalfa
Caustic
Epistle
Gateleg
Ingrain
Intrude
Natural
Raiding
Scanner
Stating
Triplet

9 letters
Affronted
Amaryllis
Arduously
Assurance
Dictating
Etiquette
Interrupt
Oversteer
Pollutant
Recurrent
Tottering
Unresting

★★ One-Way Streets

The diagram represents a pattern of streets. P's are parking spaces, and the black squares are shops. Find the route that starts at a parking space, passes through all the shops exactly once, and ends at the other parking space. Arrows indicate one-way traffic for that block only. No block or intersection may be entered more than once.

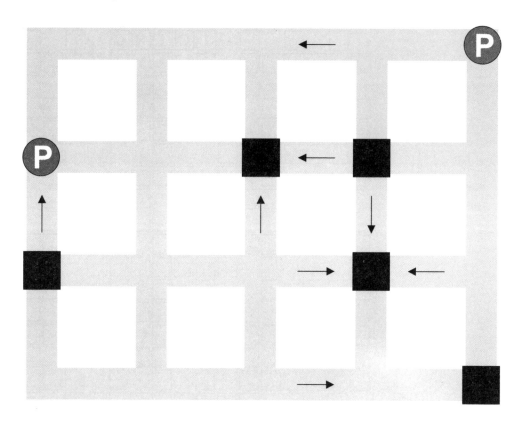

CHOP AND CHANGE

Delete one letter from the word BENDING and rearrange the rest to get a word that means harmless.

★★ **123**

Fill each blank square in the grid with the number 1, 2 or 3 so that each completed row and column has an equal number of 1s, 2s and 3s. Each bold rectangular block must contain all three numbers, and no two horizontally or vertically adjacent squares may contain the same number.

	1				3		
			1				
1							2
		2					
				2			
3							
						3	
	2						1
		1		3			

SUDOKU SUM

Write a digit from 0-9 in each of the five blank spaces to make a calculation that works. No digit may be repeated in the sum.

```
  _ 4 9
+ 1 _ _
-------
  7 _ _
```

★★★ Line Drawing

Draw three straight lines, each from one edge of the square to another edge, to create five regions, each one containing numbers that total more than 25, but less than 35.

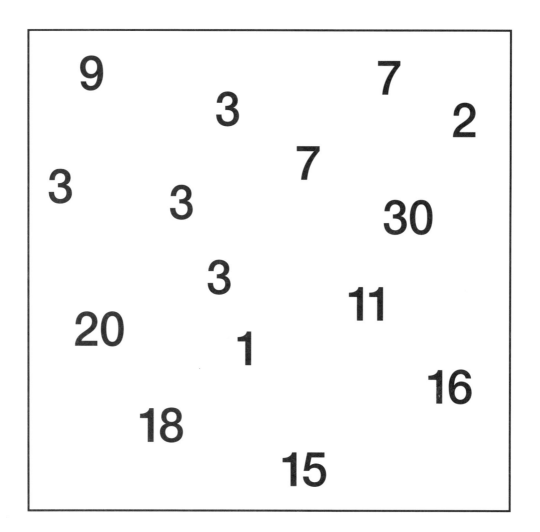

THREE OF A KIND

Find three hidden words in the sentence that, read in order, go together in some way.

Once in the van, I'll ask the policeman not to scream at him.

★★★ Number Jig

Fit all the listed numbers into the grid. One number is already in place to help you get started.

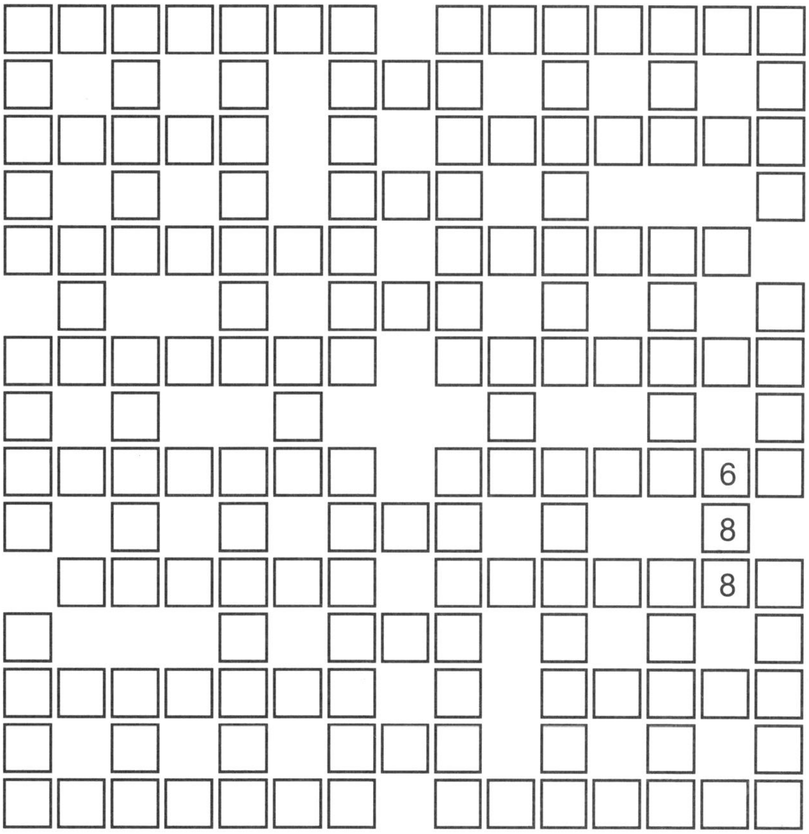

3 digits
110
167
184
368
567
583
634
671
676
~~688~~
714
732

4 digits
2107
6173
8178
8693

5 digits
13522
41242
61556
78176
82741
87282
91241
97636

6 digits
524701
902884

7 digits
1075636
1336462
1417963
1575457
3132721
5250887
6350126
6350941
6618276
6621487
6767168
7084807
7274253
8060428
8145812
8476408
9020849
9511277
9618889
9745762

★★ Star Search

Find the stars that are hidden in some of the blank squares. The numbered squares indicate how many stars are hidden in the squares adjacent to them (including diagonally). There is never more than one star in any square.

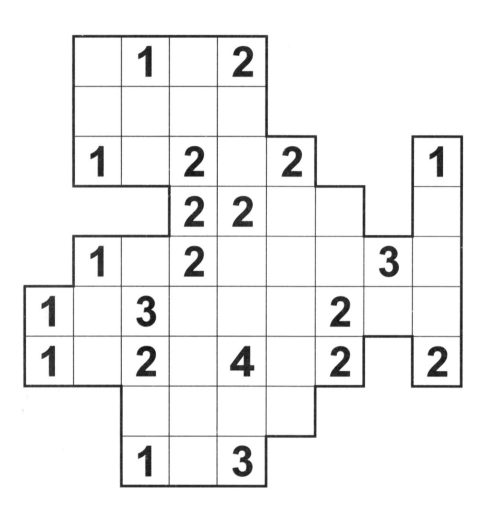

TELEPHONE TRIOS

Using the numbers and letters on the telephone keypad, what three seven-letter words, names or phrases on a common theme can be formed from the numbers below?

6682253 _ _ _ _ _ _ _

7732425 _ _ _ _ _ _ _

8687825 _ _ _ _ _ _ _

	ABC	DEF
1	2	3
GHI	JKL	MNO
4	5	6
PRS	TUV	WXY
7	8	9
*	0	#

★★ Tri-Colour Maze

Enter the maze at the bottom right, pass through all the coloured squares exactly once and then exit at the bottom left, all without retracing your path. You must pass through the coloured squares in this sequence: yellow, blue, red, yellow, blue, red etc.

RHYMING TRIO

Rearrange the listed letters to form three one-syllable words that rhyme.

B D E G H L O O O U W W

_____ _____ _____

★★★ Skeleton Crossword

FULL SYMMETRY PATTERN

Using the clue numbers and black squares already in the grid to get you started, fill in the black squares as well as the answers to complete this crossword. The grid follows a fully symmetrical pattern.

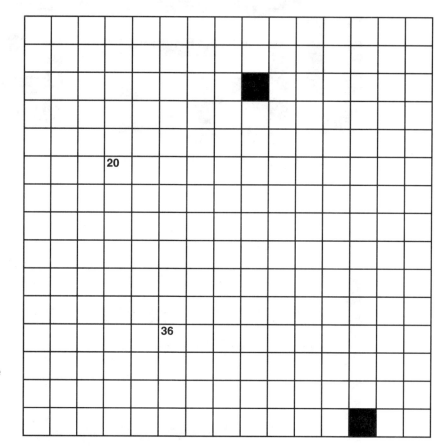

ACROSS

- **8** Mexican currency
- **9** Dr Manmohan ___, prime minister of India
- **10** Plunder
- **11** Zero
- **12** Freeze over
- **13** Landlocked country of central Africa
- **15** Narcotic obtained from poppies
- **16** Squirrel's nest
- **18** Dishonest scheme
- **21** First digit
- **23** Rooster
- **25** Vanity
- **26** Ivy League university
- **28** Continent bordered by the Ural mountains
- **30** ___ Richards, Rolling Stones guitarist
- **31** Nub, gist
- **33** Dangled
- **36** Sag
- **38** Funeral heap
- **40** Will Smith boxing film
- **41** Saudi Arabia's most important export
- **42** Pepper grinder
- **43** Interior colour scheme
- **44** Mormon state of the USA

DOWN

- **1** Fine net
- **2** Firm tie
- **3** Scandinavian capital city
- **4** Fearful
- **5** Passing fancy
- **6** Snow vehicle
- **7** Interlaced
- **14** Turkish ruler
- **17** Spanish word for 'river'
- **19** Traverse
- **20** Islam's holiest city
- **21** Broad or dense
- **22** Sandy shore
- **23** Municipal
- **24** Greek island near Albania
- **27** Dissolution of marriage
- **29** Electrically charged particle
- **32** ___ Lichtenstein, US Pop artist
- **34** Single entity
- **35** Cheek, impudence
- **36** Carthaginian queen loved by Aeneas
- **37** Sweat gland opening
- **38** Purple fruit with a stone
- **39** Highway

★★ Hyper-Sudoku

Fill in the empty cells so that every row, column, 3x3 block and each of the four 3x3 grey regions contains all of the digits from 1-9.

								8
		3	6					
6	2	4	9					
		8		7		3	2	
					5	8	1	4
	9				2			7
		5		1		9		
	4		2					
						2		3

TAKE TWO

Take two consecutive letters from each of the three words, in order, to spell a six-letter word.

YOGA LAMB COOL ☐☐ ☐☐ ☐☐

★★ ABC

Enter the letters A, B and C into the diagram so that each row and column has exactly one A, one B and one C, leaving two blank boxes in each row and column. The letters outside the diagram indicate the first letter encountered, moving in the direction of the arrow.

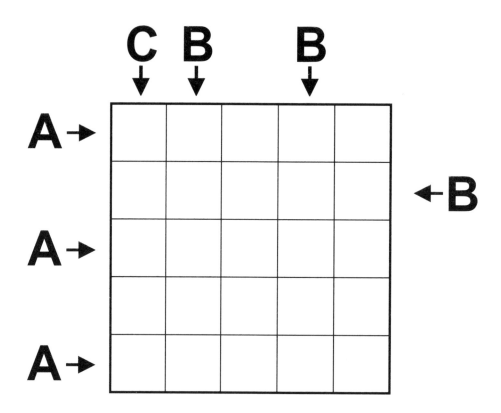

CLUELESS CROSSWORD

Complete the crossword with common seven-letter words, not using names (proper nouns), based entirely on the letters already filled in for you.

★★★ Codeword

Can you crack the code and complete the grid? Each letter of the alphabet appears at least once in the grid, and is represented by the same number throughout. The letters we've decoded should help you to identify other letters and words in the grid. If you would like a third starter letter, turn to page 255.

	7		15		10		7	9	3		12		26	
8	21	7	6	14	3	4	26		25	19	21	25	16	26
	26		14		25		26		13		6		19	
11	4	12	3	6	26	4		1	2	11	8	16	19	2
													I	**F**
	25		16		16		15				12		4	
14	3	7	12	18	25	26	4	26		8	17	16	21	26
16		9			8		22		8			26		21
10	7	22	10		7	3	26	4	21		12	3	25	2
7		4			21		25		6			4		25
8	7	21	12	17		6	22	16	1	15	4	26	4	26
	6		3				8		15		2		22	
4	8	17	16	12	25	3		21	4	24	4	22	10	4
	19		20		23		25		8		19		25	
24	16	11	6	25	3		15	21	4	5	6	26	10	4
	8		4		4	25	8		26		3		4	

A B C D E ̸F G H ̸I J K L M N O P Q R S T U V W X Y Z

1	2	3	4	5	6	7	8	9	10	11	12	13
14	15	16	17	18	19	20	21	22	23	24	25	26
		I			**F**							

★★ Wheels and Cogs

When the wizard turns his cog, towards which frog will the pointer move?

BETWEENER

What five-letter word can be inserted between the two words below to make a well-known expression with each?

CORK __ __ __ __ __ DRIVER

★★ Find the Ships

Determine the position of the 10 ships listed on the right of the grid; one piece has been inserted in the grid to get you started. The ships may be oriented either horizontally or vertically. A square with wavy lines indicates water and will not contain part of a ship. The numbers at the edge of the grid indicate how many squares in that row or column contain parts of ships. When all 10 ships are correctly placed in the grid, no two of them will touch each other, not even diagonally.

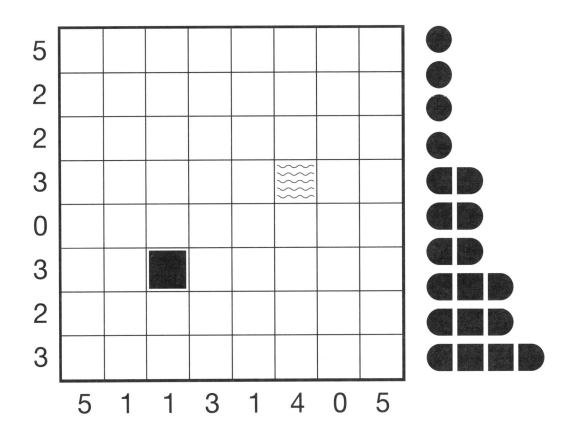

BRAINSTRETCHER

Choose the lettered answer that best copies the pattern of the first link. Some lateral thinking is required.

Charles de Gaulle is to *Paris*, as *Leonardo da Vinci* is to:

(a) Milan (b) Venice (c) Florence (d) Rome

★★ Triad Split Decisions

In this crossword without clues, each answer consists of two words that share common letters, but diverge into different words through the consecutive letters given. All answers are common words; no proper nouns (names), phrases or hyphenated words are used. More than one word pair may fit a particular section of the grid, but only one of the pairs will correctly link up with all the other word pairs.

SUDOKU SUM

Write a digit from 0-9 in each of the five blank spaces to make a calculation that works. No digit may be repeated in the sum.

$$
\begin{array}{r}
\_\ 7\ \_ \\
+\ 5\ \_\ 3 \\
\hline
\_\ \_\ 2
\end{array}
$$

★★★ Crossword

ACROSS

1 Tree of the willow family (6)
4 Vague (7)
10 Sweet lump for tea and coffee (5,4)
11 Sign of the zodiac, the Scales (5)
12 Propagator (7)
13 Deflected (7)
14 Indolent (4)
15 The Orient (4)
17 Astound (4)
21 Impolite (4)
22 Europe's highest volcano (4)
23 Dash, flair (4)
26 Pattern on stockings (7)

29 Card game related to rummy (7)
30 Remains of a felled tree (5)
31 Swiss cowherds' instrument (9)
32 Curvaceous (7)
33 Political shelter (6)

DOWN

1 Overlook, disregard (4,2)
2 Obstinate (3-6)
3 Edited, cut (8)
5 Electronic sound (5)
6 Long crunchy salad stick (6)
7 Jewish holy man (5)
8 Nourishing substance (8)

9 Small oily fish (7)
16 Nautical painting (8)
18 Mushroom-like fungus, often poisonous (9)
19 Declare openly (7)
20 Hills forming the backbone of England (8)
24 Quickly take advantage of (4,2)
25 Double-size champagne bottle (6)
27 ___ *Pacific*, musical (5)
28 Drag a fishing net (5)

 **123**

Fill each blank square in the grid with the number 1, 2 or 3 so that each completed row and column has an equal number of 1s, 2s and 3s. Each bold rectangular block must contain all three numbers, and no two horizontally or vertically adjacent squares may contain the same number.

1						3		
		3			1			
2								1
		3				2		
								2
				3				
3							3	

CHOP AND CHANGE

Delete one letter from the word SPACIOUS and rearrange the rest to get the last name of a famous artist.

_____

★★ Fences

Connect adjacent dots with vertical or horizontal lines, so that a single loop with no crossings or branches is formed in the grid. Each number indicates how many lines surround it. Square spaces with no number may be surrounded by any number of lines.

ADDITION SWITCH

Switch the positions of two of the digits in this incorrect sum to make a calculation that works.

```
  7 8 4
+ 1 9 2
-------
  5 3 6
```

★★★ Alphabetical Crossword

Each answer in this crossword begins with a different letter of the alphabet. You must solve the clues and decide where each answer belongs in the grid.

A _____

B _____

C _____

D _____

E _____

F _____

G _____

H _____

I _____

J _____

K _____

L _____

M _____

N _____

O _____

P _____

QUARTO _____

R _____

S _____

T _____

U _____

V _____

W _____

X _____

Y _____

Z _____

- Huge (4)
- Baby kangaroo (4)
- Area, sector (4)
- Magician's rod (4)
- Shout (4)
- Elephant's ivory tooth (4)
- Crook's false name (5)
- Frequently (5)
- ___ *Trouper*, Abba No.1 single (5)
- Specific skill or ability (5)
- Paper size (6)
- Italian town square (6)
- Mislaying (6)
- Gently fall asleep (3,3)
- Slavers, slobbers (6)
- ___ *Ted*, sitcom about Irish priests (6)

- Case in point (7)
- Brochure, pamphlet (7)
- Dog of mixed breed (7)
- Scruffy, dishevelled (7)
- Level to which a skirt hangs (7)
- Softens, shows mercy (7)
- Vehicle used to salt icy roads (7)
- *Indiana Jones and the Last ___*, Harrison Ford film (7)
- One who plays a wooden-barred percussion instrument (11)
- Full of useful facts (11)

★★ Mask Maze

Enter the maze as indicated, pass through all the blue dots exactly once, and then exit. You may not retrace your path.

LOGICAL

See if you can solve this mini logic problem in your head before writing anything down.

West Ham, Fulham and Chelsea played important FA Cup ties on Saturday, but all kicked off at different times – 13:30, 15:00 and 17:15. Fulham kicked off at 15:00 but didn't play against Aston Villa. West Ham played Hull City and kicked off earlier than Aston Villa. Which team did Newcastle play?

Brain Breather

Nine Men's Morris – the oldest game?

Nine Men's Morris is certainly one of the world's oldest board-games. It is possible that the ancient Egyptians played it – a carved stone slab resembling a Nine Men's Morris board was found in a temple near Luxor dating back to 1400BC. We know that the game was popular in Roman times because board patterns have been found carved into Roman buildings. Evidence of ancient boards scratched into the ground has been found as far afield as Sri Lanka and the southwestern USA.

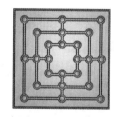

Nine Men's Morris is a game of strategy for two players. The board features three concentric squares that are linked by four straight lines, resulting in 24 intersections.

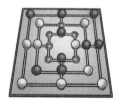

Each player starts with nine counters, or men (originally these would have been pebbles), and they take it in turns to position them one at a time on the board until all the men are in place.

Players then take turns to move their men, one at a time, onto adjacent vacant intersections, the aim being to form a row of three men, called a mill. When a player achieves a mill, he or she takes one of the opposing player's men from the board. The first player to end up with fewer than three men loses the game.

The game was popular in medieval England, where it was played on village greens and indoors. If you visit Westminster Abbey or Canterbury Cathedral, you will see game boards carved into cloister seats, suggesting that it was popular with monks.

It is not known for certain where the name *Morris* came from. One theory holds that it comes from the Latin word *merellus*, meaning a counter or gaming piece; indeed, alternative names for the game include *Merels* and *Merrills*. Or it might be related to Morris dancing, from a perceived similarity between the pattern made by the dance steps and the game moves. *Morris* in the term *Morris dancing* comes from the word *Moorish*, so that might hint at North African origins for the game – which is consistent with it being played in ancient Egypt.

As for the board pattern itself, a square within a square within a square is an ancient sacred symbol. The four straight lines could represent the four elements of the ancient world – air, fire, earth and water – or the four cardinal points of the compass, leading to the centre, called the Holy Mill, which symbolises regeneration.

Nine Men's Morris is still popular. These days you can play it online and there are numerous internet forums and groups devoted to the game.

★ Wordsearch – Eye of the Tiger

Find the 20 listed terms to do with tigers, hidden in the grid. They may read horizontally, vertically or diagonally, and either backwards or forwards. There's one additional unlisted word on the theme to be found in the diagram. Hint: it's a plural noun. Can you spot it?

Asia
Attack
Bengal
Big cats
Black
Claws
Cubs
Endangered
Growl
Hunting
India
Orange
Paws
Predator
Prowl
Roar
Species
Teeth
Territorial
Tiger

L	G	N	I	T	N	U	H	S	S	S	V
R	A	O	R	M	T	K	R	W	W	P	T
S	I	I	R	B	C	P	O	A	A	E	A
T	D	W	R	A	R	C	T	L	P	C	C
R	N	K	T	O	N	O	A	C	H	I	G
I	I	T	W	R	T	G	D	T	X	E	I
P	A	L	P	A	Y	I	E	F	J	S	B
E	N	D	A	N	G	E	R	E	D	E	C
S	H	I	S	A	T	R	P	R	N	R	U
K	C	A	L	B	I	G	O	G	E	I	B
B	I	G	C	A	T	S	A	W	S	T	S
T	I	G	E	R	D	L	A	E	L	L	U

LOOK HEAR

Can you name and spell these 3 homophones (words that sound the same but have different meanings) from the definitions given?

Example: couple; trim with a knife; bulbous fruit
Answer: PAIR, PARE, PEAR

feeling of resentment; summit; quick look

★★ Hyper-Sudoku

Fill in the empty cells so that every row, column, 3x3 block and each of the four 3x3 grey regions contains all of the digits from 1-9.

		8				1		
						4		
					1			6
9		4			6			
				1				8
	6					9		5
	7					2	3	1
3	9		1					4
		6			9	3		2

MAKE TRACKS

Lay the 'sleepers' of the track by writing the answers to the clues in the numbered Down spaces. Then work out the two 'rail' answers, reading across. The 'rail' answers, which are not necessarily single words, are to do with liberty.

1 **Fill, permeate**
2 **Powdered tobacco for inhaling**
3 **Essential**
4 **Afterwards, subsequently**
5 **Trivial, small-minded**

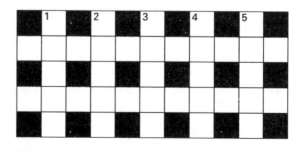

★★ Pieceword

Fit the blocks together in the empty grid to complete the crossword. Answers to the Across clues fit somewhere in the row with that number. The grid follows a fully symmetrical pattern.

FULL SYMMETRY PATTERN

ACROSS

1 Sparkle • Angry, furious • Item of neckwear

3 Wash in clear water • Item of value

4 Not one or the other

5 Charred • Yearned

6 Fluttered

7 Alloy used for beer tankards • Endorse

8 Below, beneath

9 Spool for winding yarn • Going astray or sinning

10 Any secreting organ

11 Hurled, flung • Place where bones connect

12 Exact copy

13 Tortilla chip • Complete accord

15 Gesture of indifference • Idly wander • Old church tax

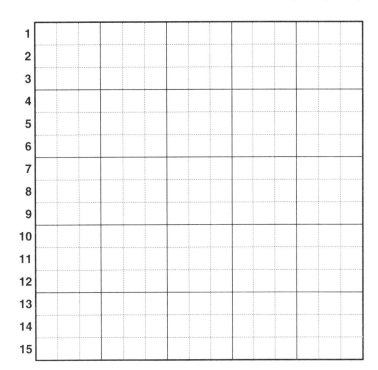

★★ One-Way Streets

The diagram represents a pattern of streets. P's are parking spaces, and the black squares are shops. Find the route that starts at a parking space, passes through all the shops exactly once, and ends at the other parking space. Arrows indicate one-way traffic for that block only. No block or intersection may be entered more than once.

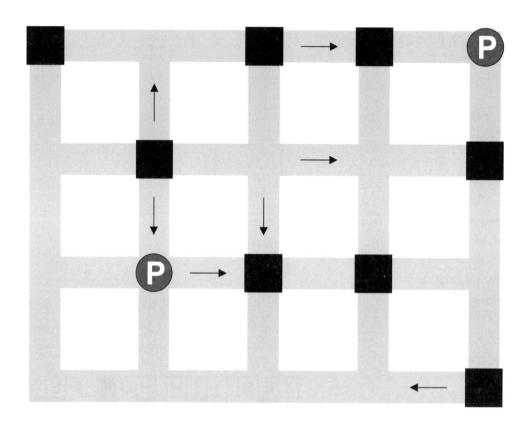

TAKE TWO

Take two consecutive letters from each of the three words, in order, to spell a six-letter word.

NEST DUPE CORN

☐☐ ☐☐ ☐☐

★★ Star Search

Find the stars that are hidden in some of the blank squares. The numbered squares indicate how many stars are hidden in the squares adjacent to them (including diagonally). There is never more than one star in any square.

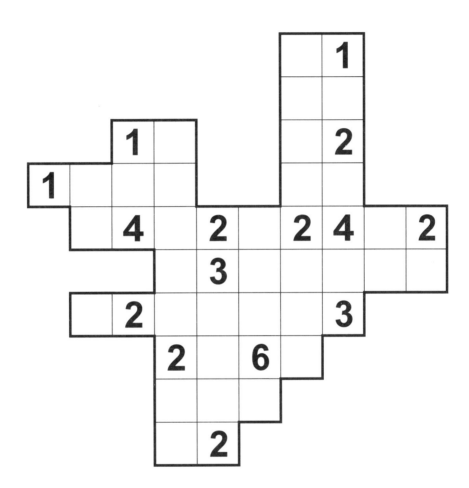

TELEPHONE TRIOS

Using the numbers and letters on the telephone keypad, what three seven-letter words, names or phrases on a common theme can be formed from the numbers below?

2428328   __ __ __ __ __ __ __

2688243   __ __ __ __ __ __ __

6267466   __ __ __ __ __ __ __

1	ABC 2	DEF 3
GHI 4	JKL 5	MNO 6
PRS 7	TUV 8	WXY 9
*	0	#

★★ Crossword

ACROSS

7 Akin (7)

8 Bitter regret (7)

9 Captured on cassette film (7)

10 Festivity, fun (7)

12 Complete halt (10)

13 Restless craving (4)

15 Slowly but surely stopping (8,2,1,4)

18 Round Dutch cheese with a red rind (4)

19 Document allowing a foreigner to be employed (4,6)

21 Crossly (7)

23 Ballast sack (7)

24 After-dinner drink (7)

25 Lay, rather than religious (7)

DOWN

1 Attended (to the wants and needs of others) (10)

2 Dabbling duck with reddish-brown plumage (6)

3 Ride behind a speedboat (5-3)

4 Breakfast food (6)

5 Stuffy, conservative (8)

6 Title of Russian emperors (4)

11 Sow farm (7)

14 Quit, give up (4,2,1,3)

16 Plenty of (8)

17 Deprived of one or both parents (8)

19 Arctic seal-like mammal (6)

20 Element discovered by Marie Curie (6)

22 Large tack (4)

★★★ Sets of Three

Group all of the symbols into sets of three, with each set having either all the same shape or all the same colour. The symbols in each set must all be connected to each other by a common horizontal or vertical side.

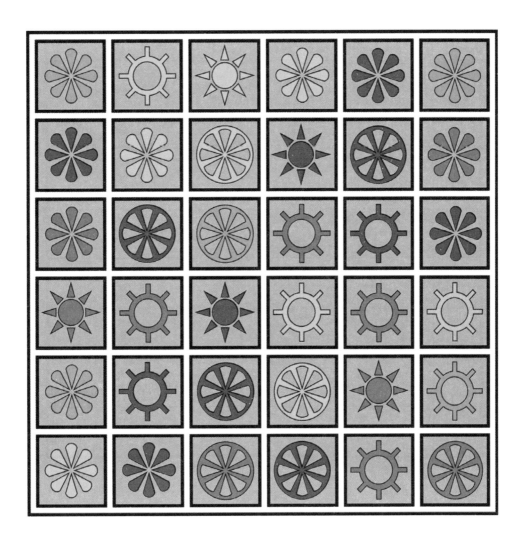

AND SO ON

Unscramble the letters in the phrase JAB DREAM to form two words that are linked by the word 'and' in a common phrase.

_____ and _____

★★ Sudoku

Fill in all the empty cells in the grid so that each row, each column and each 3x3 block contains all the digits from 1-9.

		1				4		
		8	2		9	3		
5	4			1			6	2
	5						4	
		9		5		6		
	1						2	
2	3			6			9	7
		7	4		5	1		
		5				2		

BACK NUMBERS

Starting from the mystery number, calculating each step in turn from left to right will result in the answer given. Work the sum backwards to find that missing first number.

?	treble it	double it	x 2	÷ 3	+ 19	= 71

★★ Look Both Ways Crossword

Enter your answers diagonally into the grid, either angled to the right or left as indicated.

TO THE RIGHT

1 Female big cat (7)
2 Creative skill (3)
3 Metal containers (4)
4 Enemy (3)
5 High quality cut glass (7)
6 Whacked, formerly for breaking school rules (5)
7 Noisy quarrel (3)
9 Female deer (3)
11 Soul, spirit (6)
13 Sorts according to quality (6)
14 Expanse of salt water (3)
16 Twitch (3)
19 Soft indoor shoe (7)
21 Euphoria (7)
24 Natural ability (5)
26 Strike sharply (3)
28 Idiot, dope (4)
29 Part of the mouth (3)
31 Light brown (3)
33 Plus (3)

TO THE LEFT

2 Help (3)
3 Group of soldiers (5)
4 Good health and conditioning (7)
5 Swindle (3)
6 Tops of waves (6)
7 Beam of light (3)
8 Dispatch (7)
10 Sodden (3)
12 Information (4)
15 Word of agreement (3)
17 Container cover (3)
18 Young cow (4)
20 Lose hope (7)
22 Sure (7)
23 Component of the alphabet (6)
25 Unwell (3)
27 Holy person (5)
30 Seed (3)
32 Armed combat (3)
34 Pea shell (3)

★★ Split Decisions

In this crossword without clues, each answer consists of two words that share common letters, but diverge into different words through the consecutive letters given. All answers are common words; no proper nouns (names), phrases or hyphenated words are used. More than one word pair may fit a particular section of the grid, but only one of the pairs will correctly link up with all the other word pairs.

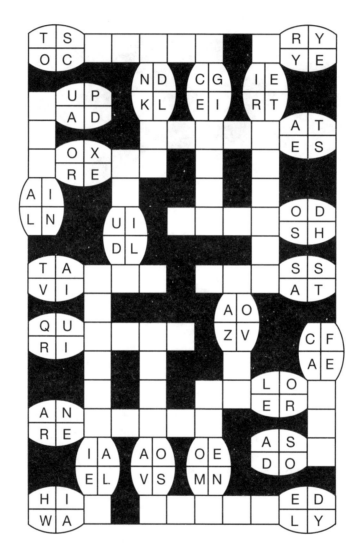

CHOP AND CHANGE

Delete one letter from the word MANICURE and rearrange the rest to get a word associated with the brain.

★★ Hitori

Black out certain squares in the grid so that no digit appears more than once in any row or column. Blacked-out squares may not touch each other horizontally or vertically, and all remaining squares must form a single continuous area.

5	6	1	6	3	5
4	5	5	6	1	5
5	2	6	6	4	3
3	3	3	4	2	6
2	6	4	5	3	1
3	4	2	1	6	4

OPPOSITE ATTRACTION

Unscramble the letters in the phrase SEAMY NEST to form two words that are opposites of each other.

_____   _____

★★★ Number Jig

Fit all the listed numbers into the grid. One number is already in place to help you get started.

3 digits
224
335
373
628
673
820
847
947

4 digits
1081
1528
2336
2668
3166
3271
3417
4069
4100
4367
5331
6188
6281
6670
7216
7877
8057
8373
9368
9748

5 digits
12198
12202
27926
38573
43026
45053
50345
51576
54233
54463
56789
81136
83453
84246
86775
92073

6 digits
107087
308336
477536
664251
770637
803015
818311
876118

★★★ ABC

Enter the letters A, B and C into the diagram so that each row and column has exactly one A, one B and one C, leaving two blank boxes in each row and column. The letters outside the diagram indicate the first letter encountered, moving in the direction of the arrow.

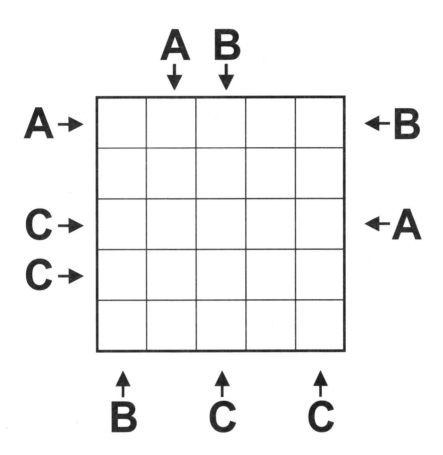

CLUELESS CROSSWORD

Complete the crossword with common seven-letter words, not using names (proper nouns), based entirely on the letters already filled in for you.

★★ Shadow Play

Which of the 12 images is the correct shadow?

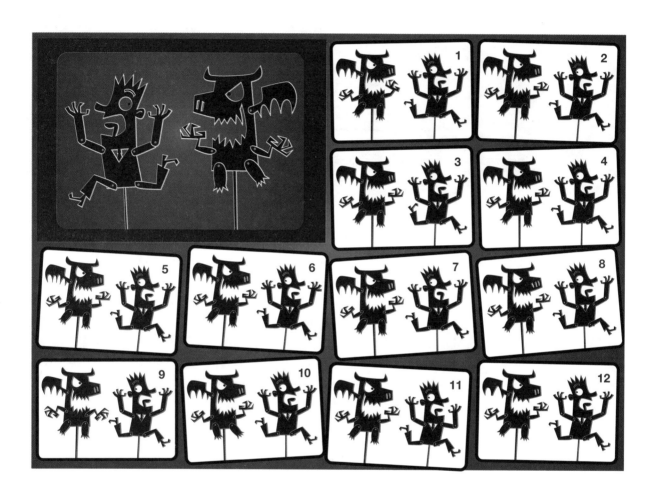

BETWEENER

What four-letter word can be inserted between the two words below to make a well-known expression with each?

OPEN __ __ __ __ WORM

★★ Line Drawing

Draw two straight lines, each from one edge of the square to another edge, to create three regions, each containing words that are related in some way. One region contains six words, one contains eight and one contains ten.

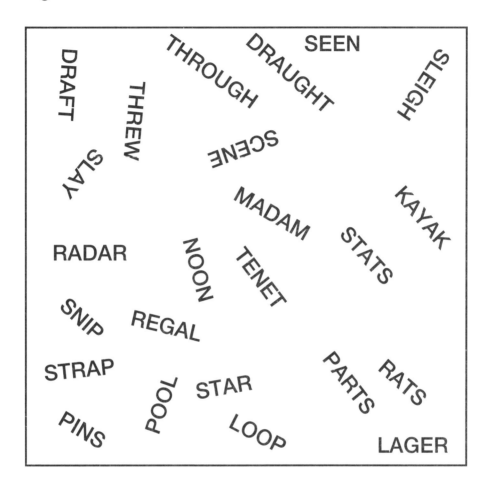

THREE OF A KIND

Find three hidden words in the sentence that, read in order, go together in some way.

Deliveries to that news stand are forbidden – is that clear now?

★★★ Skeleton Crossword

Using the clue numbers and black squares already in the grid to get you started, fill in the black squares as well as the answers to complete this crossword. The grid pattern follows central symmetry, that is, the top left corresponds to the bottom right, and the top right to the bottom left.

CENTRAL SYMMETRY PATTERN

ACROSS

1 Africa's largest country

4 Adam's second son

7 Additional tax

10 Albanian-speaking part of former Yugoslavia

12 Humiliate

13 Lily-livered

16 Swindle

18 Beard of barley or rye

19 Positive, hopeful

21 More furtive

23 French for 'friend'

24 Rascal

26 Item attached

29 Blossomed

30 Coastal motor launch

33 Artificially coloured

34 Style, manner

35 Franz ___, Czech novelist who wrote in German

DOWN

2 Mysterious aircraft

3 Commotion

5 Child-mind

6 Cheerful rhythm

7 Simple fastener

8 Treating (rubber) to increase strength

9 Keeper's area, in football

11 Take part in a winter sport

14 Virtually

15 Trained Japanese assassin

17 Sudden crisis

20 Fragment of broken glass

22 Thwarted

25 Cut (grass)

27 Nautically astern

28 Oil container

31 Infused drink

32 Largest of all living deer

★★ Find the Ships

Determine the position of the 10 ships listed on the right of the grid; one piece has been inserted in the grid to get you started. The ships may be oriented either horizontally or vertically. A square with wavy lines indicates water and will not contain part of a ship. The numbers at the edge of the grid indicate how many squares in that row or column contain parts of ships. When all 10 ships are correctly placed in the grid, no two of them will touch each other, not even diagonally.

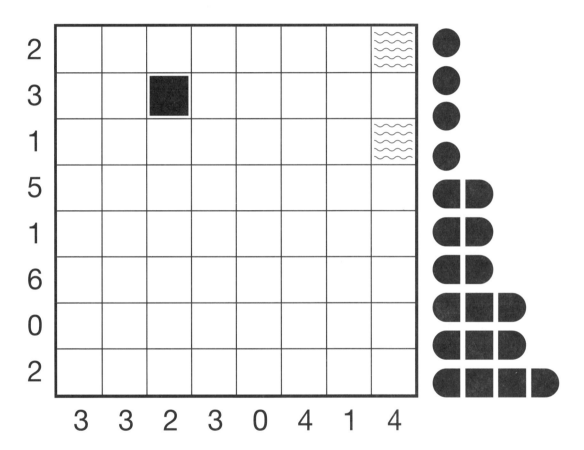

ALTER EGO

Solve the anagram contained in the bold capital letters of the clue to find the name of a celebrity. Do you know their real name?

DAINTY DEVON taxi driver

_____

★★★ Hyper-Sudoku

Fill in the empty cells so that every row, column, 3x3 block and each of the four 3x3 grey regions contains all of the digits from 1-9.

					7			
	2	7						
		4	3	8				
		6			9	3		2
4					2			1
					5	4		
	6		4					
2	5	3		6			1	
			2	7				

INITIAL REACTION

Some words of a well-known proverb or saying have been reduced to their initial letters. Can you restore the missing words?

M a T W I S in J _____

★★★ Codeword

Can you crack the code and complete the grid? Each letter of the alphabet appears at least once in the grid, and is represented by the same number throughout. The letters we've decoded should help you to identify other letters and words in the grid. If you would like a third starter letter, turn to page 255.

17		16		7		16		6		6		15		15
6	15	15	18	20	4	19		14	9	21	3	18	10 M	6 A
25		11		9		6		18		11		12		3
25	3	6	9	11		19	2	11	11	9	19	18	11	12
3		10		5		2		4		15		19		21
2	10	17	11	12	18		2	10	21	18	26	2	11	16
14		3				13		2		19				18
	26	2	9	11	14	18		4	2	16	19	2	14	
10				13		11		19				8		25
9	4	15	11	2	6	16	2		24	20	10	21	2	11
16		20		19		2		13		4		3		2
16	2	11	9	18	20	16	3	12		3	18	18	16	2
9		6		11		13		21		18		11		1
23	2	11	19	9	22	18		2	8	15	11	2	19	2
2		2		15		2		14		5		11		11

A B C D E F G H I J K L M N O P Q R S T U V W X Y Z

1	2	3	4	5	6 A	7	8	9	10 M	11	12	13
14	15	16	17	18	19	20	21	22	23	24	25	26

★★★ Fences

Connect adjacent dots with vertical or horizontal lines, so that a single loop with no crossings or branches is formed in the grid. Each number indicates how many lines surround it. Square spaces with no number may be surrounded by any number of lines.

```
3       1 2       
              3 0
   0 2            
 3         1   2
 1   3         3
           3 0
 3 3              
       0 2     3
```

ADDITION SWITCH

Switch the positions of two of the digits in this incorrect sum to make a calculation that works.

$$
\begin{array}{r}
6\,7\,7 \\
+\,2\,3\,1 \\
\hline
8\,5\,4
\end{array}
$$

★★★ Straight Ahead

Enter the grid at one of the white squares at the bottom, pass through all the green squares, then leave the grid at the lower of the two white squares on the left. You must travel horizontally or vertically in a straight line, and turn only to avoid passing through a black square. You may retrace your path, and your turns may double back as well as taking right angles.

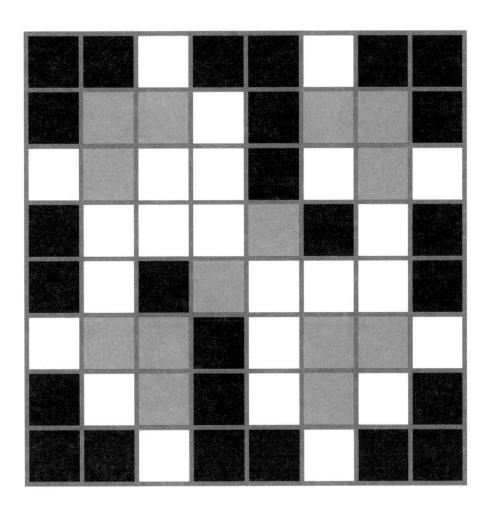

BRAINSTRETCHER

Choose the lettered answer that best copies the pattern of the first link. Some lateral thinking is required.

Europa is to *Callisto*, as *Titan* is to:

(a) Tethys (b) Phobos (c) Oberon (d) Miranda

★★ Hitori

Black out certain squares in the grid so that no digit appears more than once in any row or column. Blacked-out squares may not touch each other horizontally or vertically, and all remaining squares must form a single continuous area.

4	4	1	1	3	2
4	5	6	3	2	4
2	5	3	5	1	4
3	3	3	6	5	4
6	1	2	4	4	5
1	1	5	2	3	6

OPPOSITE ATTRACTION

Unscramble the letters in the phrase ARMY CLANG to form two words that are opposites of each other.

_____   _____

★★★ Honeycomb Crossword

All of the clues have a six-letter answer that fits around the clue's number in the grid. The number in brackets after each clue shows the segment in which the answer starts (as shown around number 1 in the grid). The answers all follow a clockwise direction.

1 Supervise, control (5)
2 Performing in a play (6)
3 Take away (3)
4 Scanty, inadequate (1)
5 Set fire to (4)
6 Deviation from a normal route (4)
7 Celestial body (1)
8 More relaxed (4)
9 Nullify (4)
10 Tool for boring holes (1)
11 Person operating a car (6)
12 Study before an exam (3)
13 Dennis the ___, comic-strip character (6)
14 Praise, recognition (6)
15 Put into cipher (1)
16 Nut used in marzipan (5)
17 Disregard (3)
18 Thief (2)
19 Stroke lovingly (6)
20 Dry material used as kindling (1)
21 Placid, obedient (5)
22 Garden plant with large bright flowers (2)
23 Area (4)
24 Illicitly influence (a jury) (5)
25 Period of teaching (5)
26 Pinched, stole (1)
27 Make up your mind (3)
28 Bargain, barter (6)
29 Larger (3)
30 Pick (5)
31 Light boats propelled with paddles (4)
32 Person who searches (5)
33 Vandalise; disfigure (1)
34 Antenna (5)
35 Relating to a clan (4)

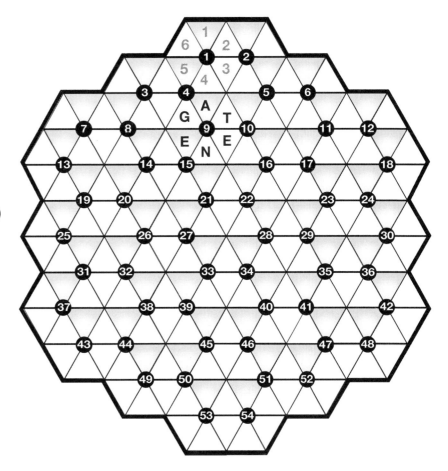

36 Continued, held out (5)
37 From one side to the other (1)
38 Tell (6)
39 Informal (1)
40 Make, bring into existence (5)
41 Checked Scottish material (5)
42 Happening unexpectedly (3)
43 Small piece (of food) (5)
44 Sofa (6)

45 Grounds of a university (2)
46 Means of entry (5)
47 Trapped (5)
48 Cleaning cloth (1)
49 Fishing equipment (1)
50 Foolishly impulsive (2)
51 Ruins (1)
52 Sags (2)
53 Changes to fit new circumstances (5)
54 Easily bent (6)

★★ Pathfinder – Tool Kit

Beginning with SPANNER (already marked), then moving up, down, left or right (never diagonally), one letter at a time, trace a continuous path in the diagram through 26 tools.

D	E	C	B	E	D	E	V	O	Y	E	E	L
R	I	A	R	P	A	L	F	H	S	K	N	L
L	L	R	S	S	T	E	I	L	A	R	W	A
T	C	E	E	N	S	H	W	E	B	M	A	S
A	N	I	P	O	T	R	T	R	W	A	L	T
P	E	I	R	O	N	E	W	O	O	R	L	E
E	M	G	P	A	N	N	E	L	V	C	R	E
A	S	N	S	D	N	I	R	G	I	C	E	M
R	U	I	R	E	A	M	P	E	N	A	H	M
E	T	D	E	R	L	C	S	L	G	E	A	A
Q	S	L	O	S	C	H	A	N	I	F	T	H
U	E	C	S	E	N	E	N	K	E	X	C	T
A	R	H	I	L	W	R	D	E	R	A	H	E

SUDOKU SUM

Write a digit from 0-9 in each of the five blank spaces to make a calculation that works. No digit may be repeated in the sum.

$$
\begin{array}{r}
\_\,2\,5 \\
+\ 7\,\_\,\_ \\
\hline
\_\,6\,\_
\end{array}
$$

★★★ Killer Sudoku

As in regular sudoku, fill all the empty cells in the grid so that each row, each column and each 3x3 block contains all the digits from 1-9. In addition, the digits in each dotted-line shape must add up to the number given in the top left corner of the shape, and no digit may be repeated within each dotted shape.

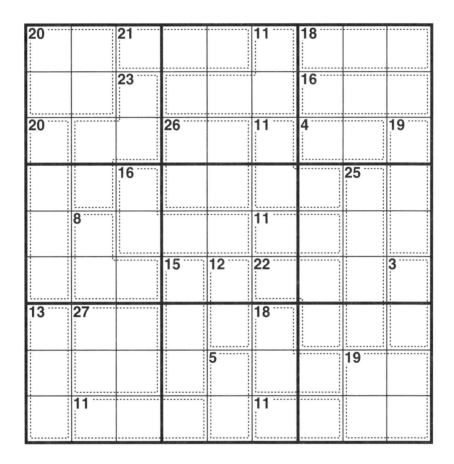

CLUELESS CROSSWORD

Complete the crossword with common seven-letter words, not using names (proper nouns), based entirely on the letters already filled in for you.

 123

Fill each blank square in the grid with the number 1, 2 or 3 so that each completed row and column has an equal number of 1s, 2s and 3s. Each bold rectangular block must contain all three numbers, and no two horizontally or vertically adjacent squares may contain the same number.

BETWEENER

What four-letter word can be inserted between the two words below to make a well-known expression with each?

TOLL __ __ __ __ RAGE

★★ Wordsearch – Creepy Crawlies

Find the 27 listed minibeasts that are hidden in the grid. They may read horizontally, vertically or diagonally, and either backwards or forwards.

Aphid
Beetle
Blowfly
Crane fly
Cricket
Earwig
Emmet
Firefly
Flea
Gnat
Grub
Hornet
Katydid
Ladybird
Leech
Locust
Maggot
Mantis
Mayfly
Midge
Moth

L	E	R	B	C	K	R	E	D	I	P	S	D	S	T
D	I	U	G	R	R	A	L	M	I	E	R	O	S	A
F	R	V	K	A	Y	H	T	O	M	I	K	U	M	S
G	X	C	E	N	L	Z	B	Y	B	E	C	Y	I	M
T	T	Q	L	E	F	W	K	Y	D	O	T	X	D	A
P	E	E	W	F	W	P	D	Q	L	I	M	J	G	Y
N	T	K	H	L	O	A	Q	V	M	J	D	D	E	F
V	B	U	C	Y	L	R	E	P	P	I	K	S	I	L
N	A	Z	I	I	B	Y	F	T	I	E	A	R	B	Y
M	R	R	H	O	R	N	E	T	A	P	E	W	L	X
M	A	G	G	O	T	C	O	R	H	F	L	Z	H	A
V	C	N	M	J	A	A	W	I	L	A	T	C	V	U
P	S	D	T	U	N	I	D	Y	C	G	E	F	H	B
S	L	U	G	I	G	M	G	N	O	E	E	L	F	C
H	X	S	W	Y	S	N	A	I	L	P	B	U	F	Q

Scarab   Slug   Spider
Skipper   Snail   Weevil

BACK NUMBERS

Starting from the mystery number, calculating each step in turn from left to right will result in the answer given. Work the sum backwards to find that missing first number.

?	x 3	- 11	÷ 4	half of it	+ 100	= 117

★★★ Looped Path

Draw a continuous, unbroken loop that passes through each of the red, blue, and white squares exactly once and avoids the black squares. Move from square to square in a straight line or by turning left or right, but never diagonally. You must alternate passing through red and blue squares, with any number of white squares in between.

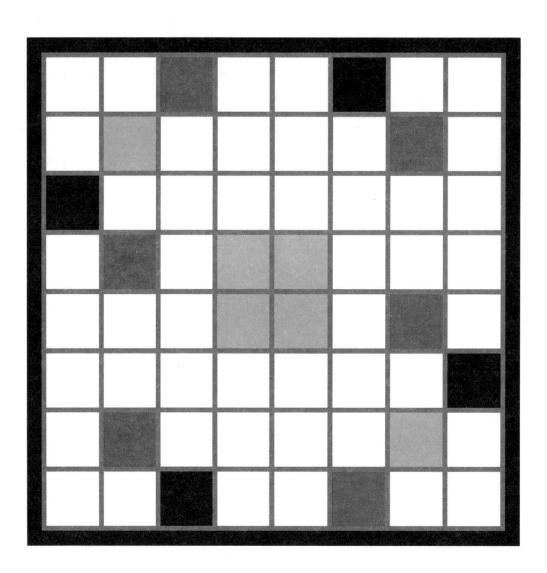

RHYMING TRIO

Rearrange the listed letters to form three one-syllable words that rhyme.

A H J O O P S T T T W

_____   _____   _____

★★ Star Search

Find the stars that are hidden in some of the blank squares. The numbered squares indicate how many stars are hidden in the squares adjacent to them (including diagonally). There is never more than one star in any square.

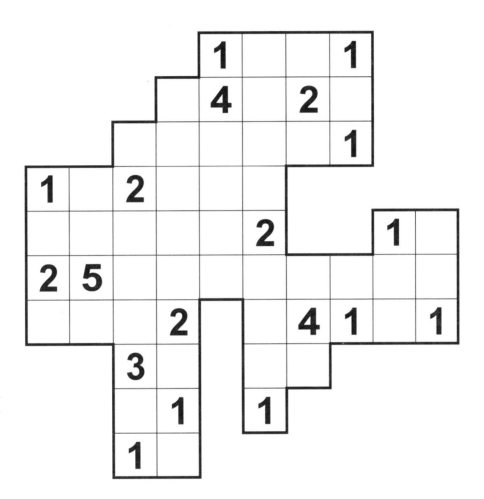

TELEPHONE TRIOS

Using the numbers and letters on the telephone keypad, what three seven-letter words, names or phrases on a common theme can be formed from the numbers below?

	ABC	DEF
1	**2**	**3**
GHI	JKL	MNO
4	**5**	**6**
PRS	TUV	WXY
7	**8**	**9**
∗	**0**	**#**

3828453   _ _ _ _ _ _ _

3527842   _ _ _ _ _ _ _

7542253   _ _ _ _ _ _ _

★★★ All in One Crossword

Single-word clues make this straight crossword a little more challenging.

ACROSS

8 Sounds (6)
9 Punctually (8)
11 Timely (9)
12 Vagrant (5)
13 Gymnast (7)
15 Twister (7)
17 Pullover (7)
18 Husbands (7)
20 Subdue (7)
23 Rub (7)
25 Expunge (5)
27 Devise (9)
29 Raised (8)
30 Elf (6)

DOWN

1 Mohair (6)
2 Scatter (8)
3 Swerve (4)
4 Fervid (6)
5 Exude (4)
6 Layers (6)
7 Manifestations (8)
10 Assemble (6)
14 Cleanse (5)
16 Rampages (5)
17 Magician (8)
18 Gloomy (6)
19 Erne (3,5)
21 Supplication (6)

22 Mellow (6)
24 Regarding (6)
26 Panache (4)
28 Atop (4)

★★★ Sudoku

Fill in all the empty cells in the grid so that each row, each column and each 3x3 block contains all the digits from 1-9.

			2		8			
3	5						2	9
		4				1		
2				6				4
			8		1			
5				2				1
		1				6		
4	3						8	7
			5		9			

MAKE TRACKS

Lay the 'sleepers' of the track by writing the answers to the clues in the numbered Down spaces. Then work out the two 'rail' answers, reading across. The 'rail' answers, which are not necessarily single words, are associated with school.

1 Gamble, bet
2 Protect from the sun
3 Fossilised resin
4 Basis of soups
5 Threaded fastener

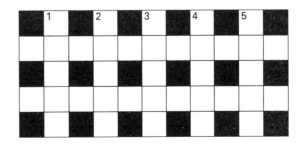

★★ One-Way Streets

The diagram represents a pattern of streets. A and B are parking spaces, and the black squares are shops. Find the route that starts at A, passes through all the shops exactly once, and ends at B. Arrows indicate one-way traffic for that block only. No block or intersection may be entered more than once.

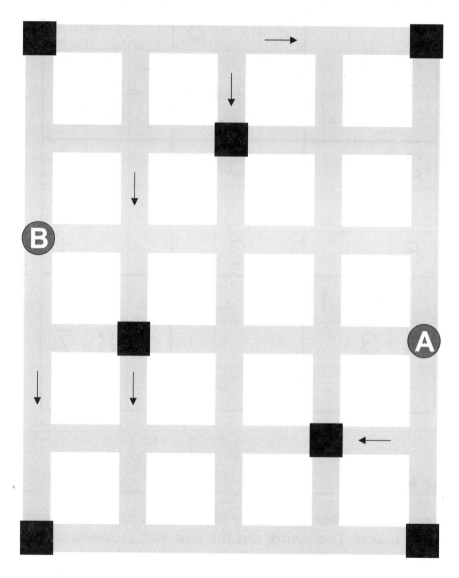

TAKE TWO

Take two consecutive letters from each of the three words, in order, to spell a six-letter word.

MUSK STOP ERGO

★★★ ABC

Enter the letters A, B and C into the diagram so that each row and column has exactly one A, one B and one C, leaving two blank boxes in each row and column. The letters outside the diagram indicate the first letter encountered, moving in the direction of the arrow.

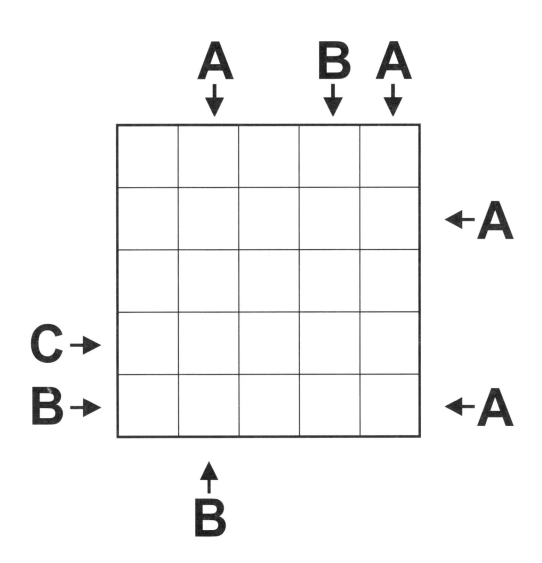

AND SO ON

Unscramble the letters in the phrase **RUSH OF BETS** to form two words that are linked by the word 'and' in a common phrase.

_____ and _____

★★ Crossword

ACROSS

9 Blundered (7,2)

10 Basket-weaving material (5)

11 Old merchants' association (5)

12 Ethereal (9)

13 Richard Branson's company (6)

15 Was of great height (7)

16 Impartial (13)

20 Whole number as opposed to a fraction (7)

22 Tacky, corny (6)

24 Flag with three stripes (9)

25 Protect (5)

26 Material often used for hosiery (5)

27 Making a long, high-pitched noise (9)

DOWN

1 Customary practice (5)

2 Spicy sauce made from chillis (4-4)

3 Mimicked (4)

4 Famous American inventor (6)

5 Fast runner (8)

6 Hazardous refuse (5,5)

7 Strong drink, spirits (6)

8 Musical overture (7)

14 Become more popular (4,6)

17 Proverbial slow-moving creature (8)

18 Over the moon (8)

19 Apt (7)

21 Insignificant thing (6)

22 Big top show (6)

23 Old saying or proverb (5)

25 Metric unit of weight (4)

★★★ Killer Sudoku

As in regular sudoku, fill all the empty cells in the grid so that each row, each column and each 3x3 block contains all the digits from 1-9. In addition, the digits in each dotted-line shape must add up to the number given in the top left corner of the shape, and no digit may be repeated within each dotted shape.

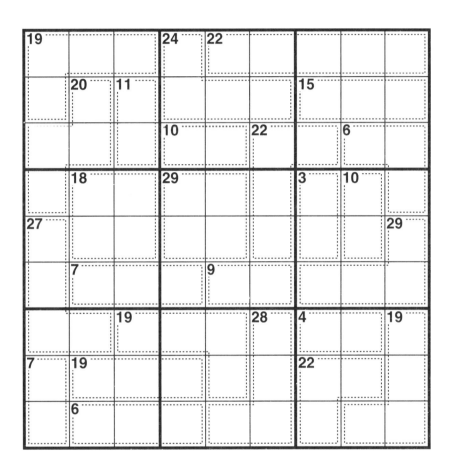

BETWEENER

What three-letter word can be inserted between the two words below to make a well-known expression with each?

CREAM __ __ __ POT

★★★ Find the Ships

Determine the position of the 10 ships listed on the right of the grid. The ships may be oriented either horizontally or vertically. A square with wavy lines indicates water and will not contain part of a ship. The numbers at the edge of the grid indicate how many squares in that row or column contain parts of ships. When all 10 ships are correctly placed in the grid, no two of them will touch each other, not even diagonally.

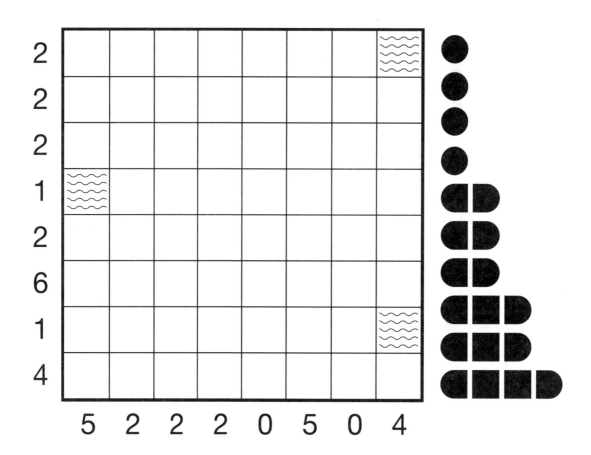

BRAINSTRETCHER

Choose the lettered answer that best copies the pattern of the first link. Some lateral thinking is required.

Nancy is to *Mr Bumble*, as *Pip* is to:

(a) Fagin (b) Uriah Heep (c) Abel Magwitch (d) Mr Pickwick

★★★ 123

Fill each blank square in the grid with the number 1, 2 or 3 so that each completed row and column has an equal number of 1s, 2s and 3s. Each bold rectangular block must contain all three numbers, and no two horizontally or vertically adjacent squares may contain the same number.

SUDOKU SUM

Write a digit from 0-9 in each of the five blank spaces to make a calculation that works. No digit may be repeated in the sum.

$$
\begin{array}{r}
2\_6 \\
+\ \_8\_ \\
\hline
\_\_5
\end{array}
$$

Brain Breather

Eye Say, Eye Say – a look at homophones

'It's not quite what I had in mind when I said 18 carats'

English is notorious for its confusing spelling. One of the drawbacks of a non-phonetic language like English is that words can look similar but sound different, as in, for example, *through*, *bough*, *trough*, *dough* and *tough*. On the other hand, variations in the spelling of sounds has resulted in many words that sound the same but are spelled differently, such as *carrot* and *carat*. This second group are called homophones, and they are a source of both great confusion and great fun.

Homophones come in pairs and trios aplenty, and there are also larger groups of them – as in *paws*, *pause*, *pores* and *pours*, for example. Variations in accent and the addition of proper nouns can swell their ranks even further – for instance, *air*, *e'er*, *err*, *heir*, *Ayr* and *Eyre*. And phrases can be homophones as well as words, as in *I scream* and *ice cream*.

The most common homophones are a source of confusion to learners of the language. How do people work out the difference between *there*, *their* and *they're*, or *to*, *too* and *two*? Reliance on computer spellcheck programs has probably exacerbated this confusion, as these confirm only that the spellings of the words in a piece of text are correct, not whether they are the correct words. A cautionary poem about spellcheckers sums up the problem:

> I have a spelling chequer
> It came with my pea see
> It highlights four my revue
> Miss steaks aye can knot sea

The compensation for these difficulties is that wayward English spelling offers enormous scope for those who like to play with language. Much British humour is based on homophones: 'What's black and white and read all over?' (a newspaper), and 'I say, I say, my wife's gone to the West Indies.' 'Jamaica?' 'No, she went of her own accord!'

Shakespeare made great use of homophones. Act II of *As You Like It* contains a play on the word *hour*. The rude joke will be lost on modern theatre-goers unless they know that *hour* and *whore* were homophones in Elizabethan times, both pronounced as *oar*.

Homophones are a regular feature of cryptic crossword clues, where their presence is indicated by a word or phrase to do with sound, such as *announced*, *aloud*, *I hear* and *so they say*. Here are some examples:

Fog avoided, we hear
    (answer: MIST, a play on *missed*)
A few lines due to be reported
    (answer: ODE, a play on *owed*)
Sheets for those singing aloud
    (answer: QUIRE, a play on *choir*)

For more fun with homophones, try the Look Hear puzzles (the first is on page 121). There are also two homophone clues in the cryptic crossword on page 180 – see if you can spot and solve them.

★★★★ Number Jig

Fit all the listed numbers into the grid. One digit is already in place to help you get started.

3 digits
120
176
211
580
636
704
753
925

4 digits
1341
1508
2288
2737
2943
3362
3813
4623
4638
5103
5200
5360
5982
7116
7744
8431
8488
8513
8548
9437

5 digits
20233
32826
40921
45561

62046
63289
67476
67515
71850
80248
80538
80824
84728
89304
90682
95655

6 digits
186786
213868
506104
511755
537772
866183
868276
938570

★★★ Fences

Connect adjacent dots with vertical or horizontal lines, so that a single loop with no crossings or branches is formed in the grid. Each number indicates how many lines surround it. Square spaces with no number may be surrounded by any number of lines.

```
2         2 2 3 2

  0 3
2       0 3
1              2
3              1
  2 3          3
    0 1
1 1 1 2        3
```

ADDITION SWITCH

Switch the positions of two of the digits in this incorrect sum to make a calculation that works.

$$\begin{array}{r} 193 \\ +875 \\ \hline 664 \end{array}$$

★★★ Hitori

Black out certain squares in the grid so that no digit appears more than once in any row or column. Blacked-out squares may not touch each other horizontally or vertically, and all remaining squares must form a single continuous area.

1	5	1	6	2	3
2	6	6	6	4	3
5	1	4	2	4	6
6	5	2	5	5	1
3	6	4	4	1	2
5	4	1	3	6	4

OPPOSITE ATTRACTION

Unscramble the letters in the phrase **VARIED HEEL** to form two words that are opposites of each other.

_____   _____

★★★ Roundabout Crossword

The five-letter answers to the Radial clues (1 to 24) read inwards from the outer edge to the centre, or outwards from the centre. Answers to the Circular clues read clockwise or anticlockwise around the circle.

Radial: Inwards

 1 Long-bladed weapon
 4 Behaved
 5 Equine creature
 6 Non-verse writing
 7 Keen, sharp
 8 Moisten (meat) with hot fat
10 Fencing weapons
13 Metric unit of liquid
15 Join together
16 Packing box
17 More secure
18 Go in
19 Hogmanay musician?
21 Lovers' meeting
22 Banquet
23 Gold bar
24 Automaton

Radial: Outwards

 2 Low humming noise
 3 Classroom tables
 9 Appears
11 Beauty boutique
12 Canonised person
14 Mistake
20 Prepared

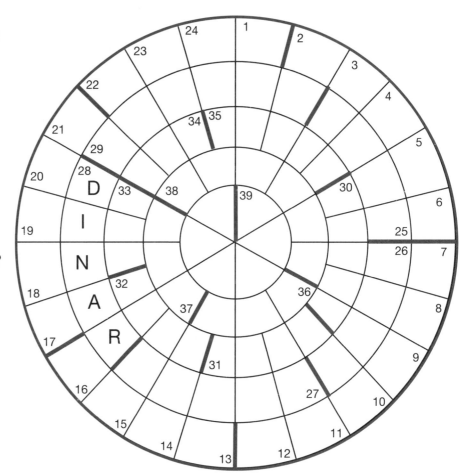

Circular: Clockwise

 7 Away
22 Cone-bearing trees
26 Sleep in a tent
27 Strong-smelling vegetable
29 Fame
30 Wake up
35 Added thrust
36 Play it by ___, improvise
37 Golf peg
38 Most tender or painful
39 Forsake, abandon

Circular: Anticlockwise

 6 Stage of development
16 Ringlet of hair
21 Sorts, kinds
25 Large boulder
28 ~~Algerian currency unit~~
31 Roof slate
32 Just, impartial
33 Suitable
34 ___ Gordons, Scottish dance

★★★ Farm Maze

Enter the maze as indicated, pass through all the blue dots exactly once, then exit. You may not retrace your path.

BETWEENER

What five-letter word can be inserted between the two words below to make a well-known expression with each?

PARKING __ __ __ __ __ READER

★★★ Hyper-Sudoku

Fill in the empty cells so that every row, column, 3x3 block and each of the four 3x3 grey regions contains all of the digits from 1-9.

8					1			
			4		8			
		9				2		8
						3		
9	6							
			1	5		4	8	
7								6
3					2			4
6	5		3		7			2

ALTER EGO

Solve the anagram contained in the bold capital letters of the clue to find the name of a celebrity. Do you know their real name?

RATTIER NUN – she's simply the best!

★ Wordsearch – Cultural Cities

Find the 24 listed cities, which have all been European City of Culture, hidden in the grid. They may read horizontally, vertically or diagonally, and either backwards or forwards.

Antwerp
Athens
Avignon
Bergen
Bologna
Bruges
Brussels
Copenhagen
Cork
Dublin
Florence
Genoa
Glasgow
Graz
Helsinki
Lisbon
Liverpool
Madrid
Paris
Porto
Prague
Salamanca
Stockholm
Vilnius

A	V	I	G	N	O	N	P	P	N	A	Z	A	R	G
K	E	S	I	P	F	R	Y	E	O	X	O	R	W	V
R	I	C	A	Q	E	Q	G	D	K	R	U	N	J	D
O	T	R	N	W	S	A	L	A	L	S	T	S	E	J
C	I	U	T	E	H	L	G	L	A	S	G	O	W	G
S	A	N	G	N	R	O	L	I	S	B	O	N	T	S
B	A	U	E	M	L	O	H	K	C	O	T	S	A	B
R	R	P	P	H	P	P	L	B	E	M	G	L	X	Z
B	O	U	V	E	A	R	O	F	A	D	A	V	Y	P
C	E	D	S	L	H	E	A	D	C	M	N	I	C	J
Z	M	U	N	S	Z	V	R	G	A	G	G	L	L	N
I	X	B	E	I	E	I	U	N	U	K	O	N	C	T
K	F	L	H	N	D	L	C	G	Y	E	L	I	W	B
N	F	I	T	K	P	A	S	W	E	O	O	U	R	Q
N	O	N	A	I	N	E	G	R	E	B	B	S	H	M

INITIAL REACTION

Some words of a well-known proverb or saying have been reduced to their initial letters. Can you restore the missing words?

T M C S the B _____

★★★★ Anagram Crossword

Unscramble the letters of the clues to get your answers. Some clues may have more than one anagram, so be sure to choose the correct one.

ACROSS

7 SATINY
8 VIPEROUS
10 ESTRANGE
11 WANING
12 PROVIDES
15 ENDEAR
16 EVIL
17 TIMER
18 SHAM
20 TESTER
22 HANDOUTS
24 NAILED
25 TEST CASE
27 CREDITOR
28 CORSET

DOWN

1 ENTAILED (4,4)
2 GRIN
3 MONDAY
4 POST
5 DECANTED
6 CINQUE
9 ORIGANUMS
13 REPULSIVE
14 GREET
17 ULTIMATE
19 CONTAINS
21 HEISTS
23 BOSSES
25 ROCK
26 ACHE

★★ Triad Split Decisions

In this crossword without clues, each answer consists of two words that share common letters, but diverge into different words through the consecutive letters given. All answers are common words; no proper nouns (names), phrases or hyphenated words are used. More than one word pair may fit a particular section of the grid, but only one of the pairs will correctly link up with all the other word pairs.

CHOP AND CHANGE

Delete one letter from the word YOUNGSTER and rearrange the rest to get a type of fish.

_____

★★★ One-Way Streets

The diagram represents a pattern of streets. A and B are parking spaces, and the black squares are shops. Find the route that starts at A, passes through all the shops exactly once, and ends at B. Arrows indicate one-way traffic for that block only. No block or intersection may be entered more than once.

LOOK HEAR

Can you name and spell these 3 homophones (words that sound the same but have different meanings) from the definitions given?

elevate; light beams; completely destroy

★★★★ Jig-a-Link

With the help of the starter letter, fit all the listed words into the grid.

3 letters
Ago
Gas
Hop
Lob
Nan
Sag
Spa
Tea

4 letters
Ache
Anon
Bust
Deli
Euro
Fail
Odds
Omen
Puny
Raid
Soda
Song
Swag
Yell

5 letters
Fiend
Fraud
Fumed
Haste
Inter
Knave
Olden
Panic
Sniff
Stuff
Taboo
Widen

Wield
Would

6 letters
Afresh
Bateau
Cuckoo
Encore
Grotto
Instep
Medium
Saluki
Stared
Voting

7 letters
Augment
Batting
Blunder
Bootleg
Concede
Copious
Economy
Embassy
Embrace
Engorge
Envelop
Grander
Inertia

Largely
Muddier
Onwards
Piously
Proudly
Renewed
Storing
Treated
Uranium

★★★ Colour Paths

Find the shortest path through the maze from the top to the centre. You must use paths in this colour order: red, blue, yellow, red, blue, yellow etc. Change path colours through the white squares. It is okay to retrace your path.

AND SO ON

Unscramble the letters in the phrase RUN MY SWAN to form two words that are linked by the word 'and' in a common phrase.

_____ and _____

★★★ Star Search

Find the stars that are hidden in some of the blank squares. The numbered squares indicate how many stars are hidden in the squares adjacent to them (including diagonally). There is never more than one star in any square.

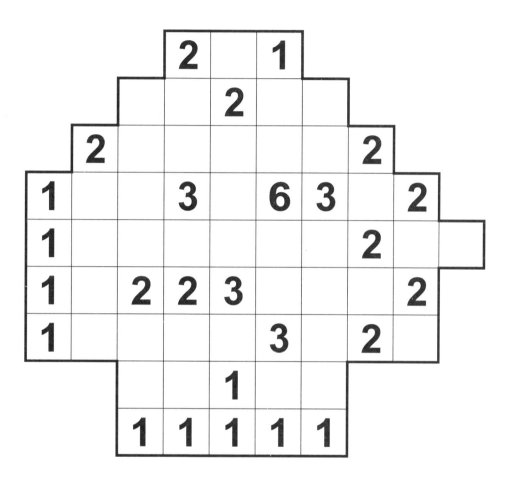

TELEPHONE TRIOS

Using the numbers and letters on the telephone keypad, what three seven-letter words, names or phrases on a common theme can be formed from the numbers below?

2325426　　＿ ＿ ＿ ＿ ＿ ＿ ＿

4625639　　＿ ＿ ＿ ＿ ＿ ＿ ＿

7888626　　＿ ＿ ＿ ＿ ＿ ＿ ＿

	ABC	DEF
1	**2**	**3**
GHI	JKL	MNO
4	**5**	**6**
PRS	TUV	WXY
7	**8**	**9**
*	**0**	**#**

★★★ Sudoku

Fill in all the empty cells in the grid so that each row, each column and each 3x3 block contains all the digits from 1-9.

1			8				5	
						8		2
	5				1		6	
9				2		7		
			3		6			
	3			4				6
	4		1			3		
8		2						
	9				2			1

THREE OF A KIND

Find three hidden words in the sentence that, read in order, go together in some way.

He was tired; didn't wait upon her

★★★ Continuity Crossword

Red lines replace black squares in this crossword to show you where words end.

ACROSS

1 Perfume • Encountered • Adds seasoning to

2 Morse ___, communication system • Royal • Mild-mannered

3 Traumatic experience • Woodwind instrument • Spring month

4 Flat-bodied fish • Perish • Use needle and thread • With no feeling

5 Horse's hoof sound • Afternoon meal • Scarlet • ___ de Janeiro, 2016 Olympics venue

6 Chaos • Drag a fishing net • Poem

7 Long sweeping cut • Belonging to that man • Enthusiastic

8 Poorly • Make fun of • Of the countryside

9 Wheel covering • Piece of farmed land • Shop selling cheese and cold cuts

10 Green gemstone • Assistance • Canine animal

11 Street plan • Region • Pinned item of jewellery

12 Smart ___, wise-guy • Trainee soldier • Thin strip of wood

13 Ceramic wall slabs • ___ Campbell, England footballer • Bellows

DOWN

1 Burn while ironing • Building location • Small rug

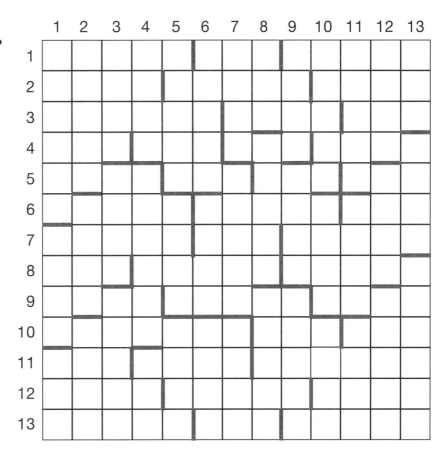

2 Marine reef growth • Friend in wartime • Timbuktu's country

3 Whirlpool • Egg-shaped • Disgust

4 Require • Paper picture on a wall • Winning tennis serve

5 Characteristic • Head cook • Parts of a circle

6 Large confused fight • Language spoken in Bangkok • Meadows

7 Overly self-regarding personalities • Get up • Decorative skirting on a wall

8 Small flap • Rub out • Fashion company's trademark

9 Sluggish • Large jug • Filthy

10 Correct • Praise highly • Quantity of medicine

11 Madagascan mammal • Man-eating giant • Child's toy figure

12 Sporting squad • Concept • Nearby pub

13 The heavens • ___ War, 1899-1902 conflict • Illuminations

★★★ ABC

Enter the letters A, B and C into the diagram so that each row and column has exactly one A, one B and one C, leaving two blank boxes in each row and column. The letters outside the diagram indicate the first letter encountered, moving in the direction of the arrow.

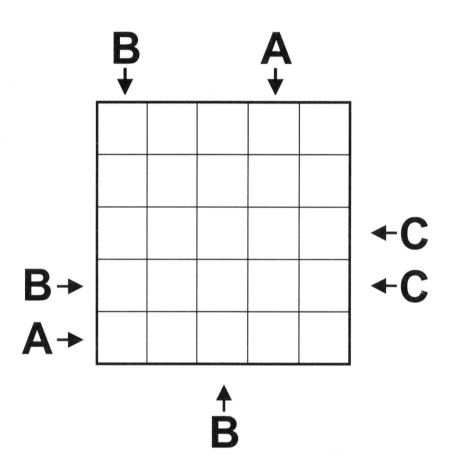

CLUELESS CROSSWORD

Complete the crossword with common seven-letter words, not using names (proper nouns), based entirely on the letters already filled in for you.

★★★ Find the Ships

Determine the position of the 10 ships listed on the right of the grid; one piece has been inserted in the grid to get you started. The ships may be oriented either horizontally or vertically. A square with wavy lines indicates water and will not contain part of a ship. The numbers at the edge of the grid indicate how many squares in that row or column contain parts of ships. When all 10 ships are correctly placed in the grid, no two of them will touch each other, not even diagonally.

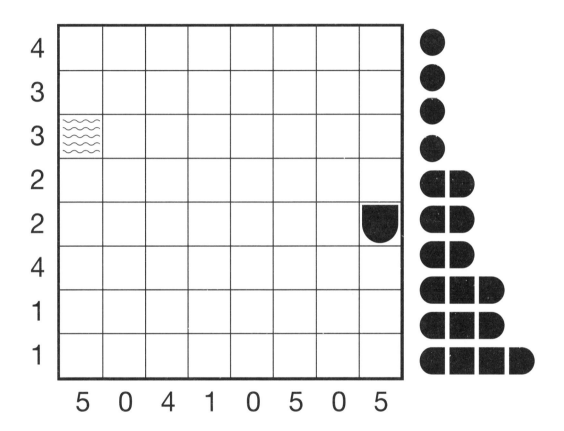

TAKE TWO

Take two consecutive letters from each of the three words, in order, to spell a six-letter word.

BEAD ROOT BAIT

★★★★ Numerical Crossword

1 Across is the place to start on this number puzzle. To clarify some of the clues, here are a few definitions: 'product' is the result of a multiplication; 'sum' is the result of an addition; 'digit total' is the sum of all the digits in the number.

ACROSS

1 The third smallest square number that could fit this space
4 One quarter of *1 Across*
6 *4 Across* plus its reverse
10 Two thirds of *18 Down*
11 Last two digits of *49 Down*
12 *5 Down* reversed
14 Five sixths of *10 Across*
15 Digit total equals *12 Across*
17 *3 Down* plus *21 Across*
19 A multiple of *1 Across*
21 First two digits plus last two digits equal *33 Across*
22 First two digits are half the last two digits
23 One quarter of the total of all answers in the top row
24 All digits are the same
26 Twice *12 Across*
27 Consecutive descending digits
29 Centre digit is the total of other two digits
31 A square number
33 One seventh of *35 Across*
35 Digit product equals *33 Across* reversed
37 *33 Across* plus *34 Down*
39 Square root of *4 Across*
40 *36 Down* plus *42 Across*
42 One and a half times *58 Down*
43 First three digits of *53 Across* minus the last three digits
46 First two digits equal half the last two digits
48 First two digits plus the last two digits equal *58 Down*
51 Digit total equals *12 Across*
53 *3 Down* plus *7 Down*
55 All digits are the same
56 Half *34 Down*
58 Five times *39 Down*
59 *29 Across* rearranged
60 Consecutive digits, not in numerical order
61 Half *48 Across*
62 First two digits plus last two digits equal *57 Down* reversed

DOWN

1 *4 Down* plus *11 Down* plus *13 Down*
2 *5 Down* plus *12 Across*
3 Consecutive digits
4 *2 Down* minus *11 Across*
5 A multiple of the digit total of *1 Across*
7 Digit total equals *39 Across*
8 Average of *4 Across* and *6 Across*
9 *27 Across* plus *24 Across*
11 *4 Across* rearranged
13 *4 Across* plus *14 Across*
16 Only two different digits used
18 Four times *26 Down*
20 Seven times *26 Across*
21 *12 Across* times *25 Down*
22 First two digits of *29 Across*
25 Last two digits of *30 Down*
26 *4 Across* plus *39 Across*
28 Average of *10 Across* and *14 Across*
30 Twice (*36 Down* reversed)
32 First digit is half the sum of other two digits
34 If multiplied by its last digit equals *52 Down*
35 First two digits equal twice last two digits
36 Half *61 Across*
37 A square number
38 Seven times (*22 Across* minus *12 Across*)
39 Half *25 Down*
41 Consecutive odd digits
44 Only two different digits used; digit total equals half the last two digits
45 Consecutive digits
47 Digit total equals twice the first digit
49 A multiple of *12 Across*
50 Digits of *26 Across* and *39 Down* rearranged
52 *4 Across* plus *12 Across* plus *58 Down*
54 Fifteen times the first two digits of *51 Across*
57 Last two digits of *52 Down*
58 *1 Across* divided by *39 Across*

★★ Patchwork

Which one of the seven patches will correctly mend the garment?

RHYMING TRIO

Rearrange the listed letters to form three one-syllable words that rhyme.

C D D D E H H I R R R T U

_____ _____ _____

★★★ **123**

Fill each blank square in the grid with the number 1, 2 or 3 so that each completed row and column has an equal number of 1s, 2s and 3s. Each bold rectangular block must contain all three numbers, and no two horizontally or vertically adjacent squares may contain the same number.

SUDOKU SUM

Write a digit from 0-9 in each of the five blank spaces to make a calculation that works. No digit may be repeated in the sum.

$$
\begin{array}{r}
7\ \_\ 9 \\
+\ \_\ 5\ \_ \\
\hline
\_\ \_\ 2
\end{array}
$$

★★★ Fences

Connect adjacent dots with vertical or horizontal lines, so that a single loop with no crossings or branches is formed in the grid. Each number indicates how many lines surround it. Square spaces with no number may be surrounded by any number of lines.

```
1 3     0   1 1
  3 1             2
3                 3
      0 1
      3 2
2                   1
3           2 2
1 2   1     1 2
```

BRAINSTRETCHER

Choose the lettered answer that best copies the pattern of the first link. Some lateral thinking is required.

Nile is to *Rhône*, as *Danube* is to:

(a) Rhine (b) Dnieper (c) Volga (d) Oder

★★★★ Cryptic Crossword

Lateral thinking, anagram skills and the ability to manipulate words and letters are what's needed to crack this cryptic crossword. There's a definition of the answer in each clue, although it may be heavily disguised.

ACROSS

1 Sent round US coin as a deposit (8)

5 Habit the shopkeeper will encourage (6)

9 Investigation could scare her terribly (8)

10 Some abhor riding – it's disagreeable (6)

12 Equality of one in a political group (6)

13 Undecided about arranging the satin (8)

15 A name is confused – because of this? (7)

16 Herb in perfect condition (4)

20 Very keen prima donna makes a comeback (4)

21 Dishonest editor follows bishop's staff (7)

25 Treading round the slope of a hill (8)

26 True, an exceptional character (6)

28 Novel item of headgear? (6)

29 Left – and that's ominous (8)

30 Unhappy tear in part of the eye (6)

31 Nears ruin in the finish – trapped (8)

DOWN

1 Fights for what's left (6)

2 'Leave pudding!' we're told (6)

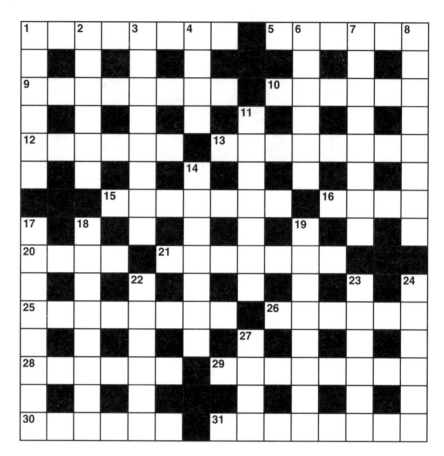

3 Not a generous period for the interval (8)

4 Family member said to be in French resort (4)

6 More perfect world (6)

7 Aquatic creature quietly found in tract of land (8)

8 Think about how to settle disputes – about time (8)

11 Meat cooking in ovens (7)

14 Deportment when carrying a burden (7)

17 Girl changing the guard (8)

18 One involved in two matches simultaneously (8)

19 Refusal country will accept, say (8)

22 Ape the historian (6)

23 Many speak but speak indistinctly (6)

24 Raised area redeveloped somewhat (6)

27 Furnace for forging link (4)

★★★ Hyper-Sudoku

Fill in the empty cells so that every row, column, 3x3 block and each of the four 3x3 grey regions contains all of the digits from 1-9.

4								
		8						
		2			6	1	7	
		6	3		7			2
						4		6
					4			
5			8	9		1		
		4				9	2	
	3			2	6		7	

ADDITION SWITCH

Switch the positions of two of the digits in this incorrect sum to make a calculation that works.

$$\begin{array}{r} 2\,1\,5 \\ +\,3\,7\,2 \\ \hline 6\,8\,8 \end{array}$$

★★★ Split Decisions

In this crossword without clues, each answer consists of two words that share common letters, but diverge into different words through the consecutive letters given. All answers are common words; no proper nouns (names), phrases or hyphenated words are used. More than one word pair may fit a particular section of the grid, but only one of the pairs will correctly link up with all the other word pairs.

CHOP AND CHANGE

Delete one letter from the word **INARGUABLY** and rearrange the rest to get a foreign language.

★★ Crossword

ACROSS

9 Region of southern Argentina (9)
10 Not censored (5)
11 Stiff (5)
12 Recall a past event (5,4)
13 Fabric awning (6)
15 Dance energetically (3,4)
16 Humiliate (4,1,6,2)
20 Unending (7)
22 Arrangement of data in rows and columns (6)
24 Looked on (9)
25 Last Greek letter (5)
26 Female relative (5)
27 Fostering (9)

DOWN

1 Ignite (5)
2 Crucifixion marks (8)
3 Advanced in years (4)
4 Intricate, difficult (6)
5 Collapsing (6,2)
6 Vehicle's rounded chair (6,4)
7 Having eight leaves to the sheet (6)
8 Adding fuel (7)
14 Each of two people (3,7)
17 Hardliner (8)
18 Liquid pressed from certain fruit (5,3)
19 Perceiving (7)
21 Number of players in a cricket team (6)
22 Contemporary (6)
23 Tropical fruit made into chutney (5)
25 Biological egg (4)

★★★ Solitaire Poker

Group the 50 cards into ten poker hands of five cards each, so that each hand contains two pairs or better. The cards in each hand must be connected to each other by a common horizontal or vertical side. Hint: four cards in the top row are part of the same straight.

For those not familiar with poker, these are examples of the hands you can form:

Two pairs (eg K♠, K♥, 7♦, 7♥, 10♣)
Three of a kind (eg 9♠, 9♦, 9♣, A♥, 3♣)
Straight (eg 3♣, 4♥, 5♥, 6♠, 7♦)
Flush (eg K♦, J♦, 6♦, 3♦, 2♦)
Full house (eg 6♦, 6♥, 6♣, Q♠, Q♦)
Four of a kind (eg 8♠, 8♦, 8♥, 8♣, J♥)
Straight flush (eg 6♠, 7♠, 8♠, 9♠, 10♠)

★★★ Hitori

Black out certain squares in the grid so that no digit appears more than once in any row or column. Blacked-out squares may not touch each other horizontally or vertically, and all remaining squares must form a single continuous area.

4	6	5	3	2	5
3	3	6	5	4	5
5	3	5	1	4	4
2	3	3	5	6	5
6	5	4	6	3	2
1	1	4	4	5	4

OPPOSITE ATTRACTION

Unscramble the letters in the phrase **ABDUCT DARTS** to form two words that are opposites of each other.

_____   _____

★★★ One-Way Streets

The diagram represents a pattern of streets. A and B are parking spaces, and the black squares are shops. Find the route that starts at A, passes through all the shops exactly once, and ends at B. Arrows indicate one-way traffic for that block only. No block or intersection may be entered more than once.

BACK NUMBERS

Starting from the mystery number, calculating each step in turn from left to right will result in the answer given. Work the sum backwards to find that missing first number.

?	÷ 7	treble it	double it	+ 26	÷ 4	= 23

★★★ Pieceword

Fit the blocks together in the empty grid to complete the crossword. Answers to the Across clues fit somewhere in the row with that number. The grid pattern follows biaxial symmetry, that is, the left corresponds to the right, and the top to the bottom.

BIAXIAL
SYMMETRY
PATTERN

ACROSS

2 Absconding • Emitting radiance

4 Unlock • Species of owl • Short thin branch

6 Polluted air • Sceptic • Crocus bulb

8 Number of original disciples • Thoughtfully

10 Flowed from a cut • Classified • Hue

12 Hard Rock ___, international chain of US-style restaurants • Ornamental napkin • Pass over, leave out

14 Large relative of the weasel • Pound rhythmically

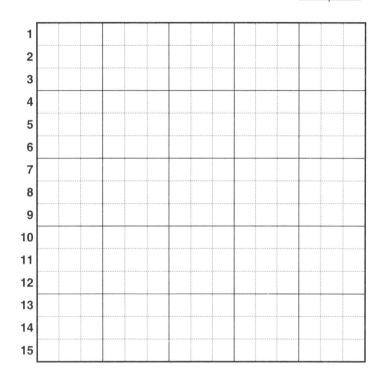

★★★ Sudoku

Fill in all the empty cells in the grid so that each row, each column and each 3x3 block contains all the digits from 1-9.

			3	8	6			
		7		4		1		
	2						6	
8								6
5	3			9			7	8
4								3
	5						2	
		9		6		4		
			2	7	4			

ALTER EGO

Solve the anagram contained in the bold capital letters of the clue to find the name of a celebrity. Do you know their real name?

Enter the Dragon – **CUE... REBEL!**

_____

★★★ Star Search

Find the stars that are hidden in some of the blank squares. The numbered squares indicate how many stars are hidden in the squares adjacent to them (including diagonally). There is never more than one star in any square.

1	1	1		2

2		4		1		1		1

TELEPHONE TRIOS

Using the numbers and letters on the telephone keypad, what three seven-letter words, names or phrases on a common theme can be formed from the numbers below?

3362464 _ _ _ _ _ _ _

5283546 _ _ _ _ _ _ _

7468788 _ _ _ _ _ _ _

1	ABC 2	DEF 3
GHI 4	JKL 5	MNO 6
PRS 7	TUV 8	WXY 9
*	0	#

★★★ Codeword

Can you crack the code and complete the grid? Each letter of the alphabet appears at least once in the grid, and is represented by the same number throughout. The letters we've decoded should help you to identify other letters and words in the grid. If you would like a third starter letter, turn to page 255.

18	14	15	14	24	8		18	16	24	13	14	12	23	
15		11		18		15		24		12		24		9
13	26	11	9 G	26 O	14	14	1	22		1	21	8	1	12
1		26		12		14		8		21		24		15
12	3	9	9	15	9	1		1	25	1	8	14	26	11
23		15		14		22				5				24
	6	22	1	1		5	24	15	12		18	4	3	22
4		8		5		1		24		8		3		9
15	19	1	14		4	1	15	11		26	6	11	15	
10			7					8		22		12		9
12	15	8	17	3	1	11		11	1	8	14	26	11	23
26		1		22		15		15		12		24		11
10	15	12	1	14		24	22	13	12	3	1	22	2	15
15		12		1		18		14		5		1		14
	14	26	5	5	12	1	11		20	1	5	5	12	1

A B C D E F G̶ H I J K L M N Ø P Q R S T U V W X Y Z

1	2	3	4	5	6	7	8	9 G	10	11	12	13
14	15	16	17	18	19	20	21	22	23	24	25	26 O

★★★ Go with the Flow

Enter the maze at the top, pass through all the circles, then exit. You must go with the flow, making no sharp turns, and may use paths and pass through circles more than once.

INITIAL REACTION

The words of a well-known proverb or saying have been reduced to their initial letters. Can you restore the missing words?

P W Y P _____

★★★ Jigsaw

Which four of the lettered pieces will complete the jigsaw to make a perfect square?

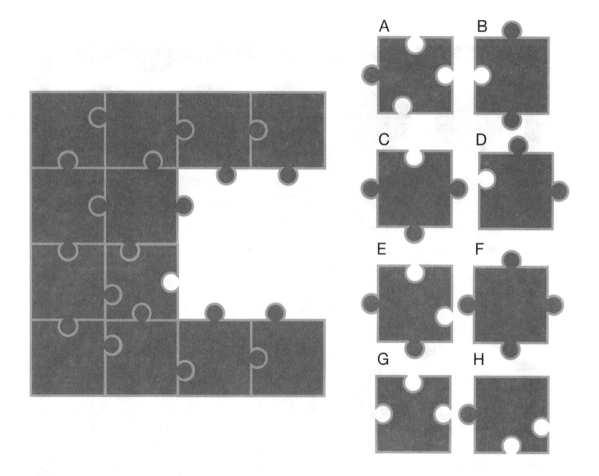

MAKE TRACKS

Lay the 'sleepers' of the track by writing the answers to the clues in the numbered Down spaces. Then work out the two 'rail' answers, reading across. The 'rail' answers, which are not necessarily single words, are nautical terms.

1 High-temperature sickness
2 Mournful poem
3 Purity unit for gold
4 Position, situate
5 Old-style hairnet

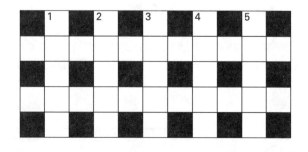

★★★ ABC

Enter the letters A, B and C into the diagram so that each row and column has exactly one A, one B and one C, leaving two blank boxes in each row and column. The letters outside the diagram indicate the first letter encountered, moving in the direction of the arrow.

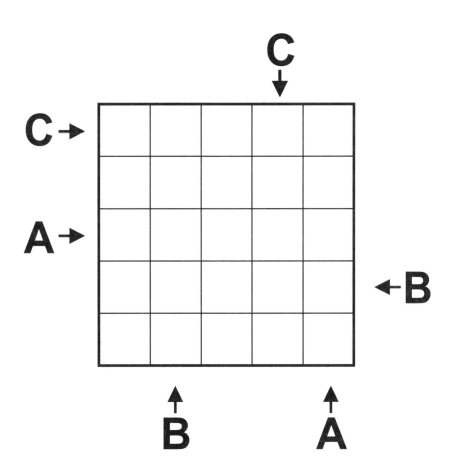

CLUELESS CROSSWORD

Complete the crossword with common seven-letter words, not using names (proper nouns), based entirely on the letters already filled in for you.

Brain Breather

Words with a Nautical Bent

England has always been a seafaring nation, so it is not surprising that many idioms in the language make reference to the sea, ships and sailing. The nautical origin of phrases such as *all at sea*, *on an even keel* and *sailing close to the wind* is evident, but there are other metaphors and expressions where the link is not so obvious.

A copper-bottomed agreement or guarantee is one that is completely reliable. The adjective *copper-bottomed* dates from the 18th-century, an age when the bottoms of wooden sailing ships were plated in copper to protect the planks from damage caused by barnacles and clams.

Chock-a-block, meaning crammed full, is another adjective with a naval origin. It refers to the block and tackle system used on ships to raise the sails. When a sail is fully raised, the two blocks are jammed closely, or chocked, together.

If you are expecting serious trouble nowadays you might *batten down the hatches*, just as sailors did when bad weather was on the way. In fine weather they would have caulked the battens – strips of wood used to fasten the hatches tightly – to make them leakproof.

Logging on to your computer might seem far removed from the sea and sailing, but this term, too, has a nautical history, as it developed from the term *log-book*. At one time sailors threw a block of wood attached to a line of rope into the sea to measure speed and distance, information which the ship's captain recorded each day in his record book or log-book.

Some phrases sound like they should have a nautical origin, but probably don't. *The bitter end*, first recorded in 1627, is one such phrase. The theory has been put forward that *bitter* refers to a turn of the rope around the bitt, a strong post firmly fixed in the deck of a ship to which cables were fastened. When the rope was played out to the bitter end, it meant that there was no rope left. Yet the adjective *bitter* meaning sour-tasting was well known to Shakespeare and earlier dramatists, and *the bitter end* is more likely to derive from this usage.

Many believe that *cat* in the phrase *no room to swing a cat* refers to the on-board whip, cat o'nine tails, but written evidence of the whole phrase has been found which predates the first appearance in print of *cat o'nine tails*. Yet another nautical origin scuppered! It is because of examples such as these that a bemused etymologist invented a spoof organisation called CANOE – the Committee to Ascribe a Naval Origin to Everything.

★★★ Crossword

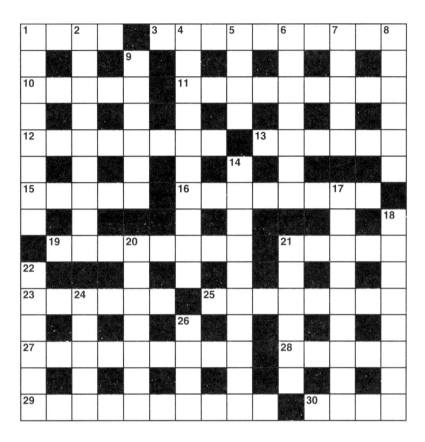

ACROSS

1 Aromatic spice (4)

3 Worried, upset (10)

10 Pertaining to the organ of smell (5)

11 Without a legal will (9)

12 National border (8)

13 Large hole in the ground (6)

15 Descendant, offshoot (5)

16 Sangfroid (8)

19 Relating to the time of year (8)

21 Red ___, oil-well firefighter (5)

23 County of Northern Ireland, capital Belfast (6)

25 Bewildered (8)

27 With a hangdog expression (4-5)

28 Happening, brewing (5)

29 Open, without deception (5,5)

30 Go off at a tangent (4)

DOWN

1 Ugly but edible sea creature (8)

2 Alter to suit (9)

4 Showing luminous colours (10)

5 Large modern-art gallery in London (4)

6 Loser, nonentity (4-3)

7 Corruption (5)

8 Hypothetical reasoning (6)

9 Nitrogenous substance in wheat (6)

14 Global politics (5,5)

17 Soft rock consisting largely of talc (9)

18 Hunter (8)

20 1950s musical style of which Lonnie Donegan was 'king' (7)

21 Disturbance (6)

22 Spanish seafood and rice dish (6)

24 Argentinian ballroom dance (5)

26 Nymph who loved Narcissus (4)

★★★ Find the Ships

Determine the position of the 10 ships listed on the right of the grid; one piece has been inserted in the grid to get you started. The ships may be oriented either horizontally or vertically. A square with wavy lines indicates water and will not contain part of a ship. The numbers at the edge of the grid indicate how many squares in that row or column contain parts of ships. When all 10 ships are correctly placed in the grid, no two of them will touch each other, not even diagonally.

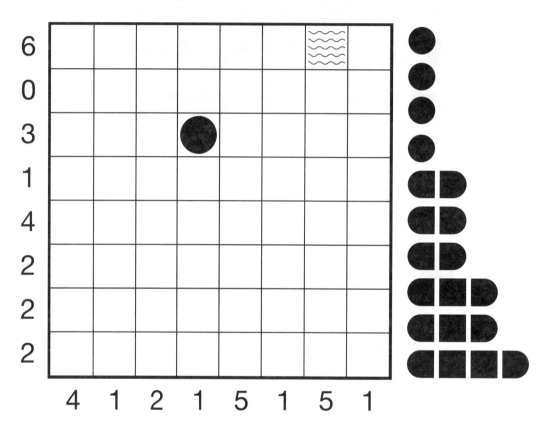

AND SO ON

Unscramble the letters in the phrase OF USA, SURF IT to form two words that are linked by the word 'and' in a common phrase.

_____ and _____

★★★ Hyper-Sudoku

Fill in the empty cells so that every row, column, 3x3 block and each of the four 3x3 grey regions contains all of the digits from 1-9.

					5		1	
	1	2						
		9		8	4			
	7						9	
1	5			6		3	7	
4		9						
	8							
3			6			7		

BETWEENER

What five-letter word can be inserted between the two words below to make a well-known expression with each?

SCARLET __ __ __ __ __ PITCH

★★★ Skeleton Crossword

Using the clue number and black square already in the grid to get you started, fill in the black squares as well as the answers to complete this crossword. The grid follows a fully symmetrical pattern.

ACROSS

1 Principal goddess of ancient Egypt
4 Cry fitfully
6 Religious ceremony
10 Indian unleavened loaf
11 West African republic
12 Sworn vow
13 Serpent
14 Adroit
17 Chief Roman god
18 Relating to movement
20 Walked upon
23 Thin and bony
25 Variegated
26 Final state of insect life
27 Small particle
31 Papal state
32 Giant Sequoia
33 Song of praise
34 Top cover
35 Brief letter

DOWN

2 Found, initiate (two words)
3 Oscillate
4 Specialist bowler
5 Capital of Thailand
6 Baltic capital
7 Flood
8 Radio code word between delta and foxtrot
9 Makeshift boat
15 Musical exercise
16 Vicious growl
17 Protrude
19 Flirtatiously modest
21 For all to see
22 Symbolic, token
23 Sweetened
24 Lacking
25 Lay slabs
28 Devised
29 Cast an eye over
30 Supreme Norse god

★★★★ Killer Sudoku

As in regular sudoku, fill all the empty cells in the grid so that each row, each column and each 3x3 block contains all the digits from 1-9. In addition, the digits in each dotted-line shape must add up to the number given in the top left corner of the shape, and no digit may be repeated within each dotted shape.

RHYMING TRIO

Rearrange the listed letters to form three one-syllable words that rhyme.

A E K K K L O O O P S S Y

_____   _____   _____

★★★★ Fences

Connect adjacent dots with vertical or horizontal lines, so that a single loop with no crossings or branches is formed in the grid. Each number indicates how many lines surround it. Square spaces with no number may be surrounded by any number of lines.

```
1 1   1 0 2   2

1           3     3
                2
      3
  1       3         1
  2
  1   3 1 2   2 3
```

ADDITION SWITCH

Switch the positions of two of the digits in this incorrect sum to make a calculation that works.

```
  3 0 5
+ 1 7 4
-------
  9 8 4
```

★★★ First Thoughts

Each answer in this grid is a word or phrase that can precede the clue word to make a well-known word or expression.

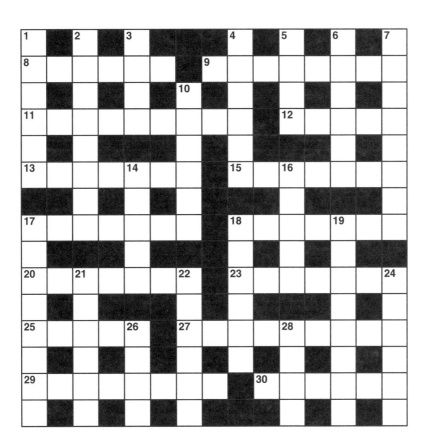

ACROSS

8 ___ ticket (3-3)
9 ___ youth (8)
11 ___ Army (9)
12 ___ supreme (5)
13 ___ -glass (7)
15 ___ Pensioner (7)
17 ___ story (7)
18 ___ circumstances (7)
20 ___ jacket (7)
23 ___ tiles (7)
25 ___ -Royce (5)
27 ___ polish (9)

29 ___ mining (4-4)
30 ___ Convention (6)

DOWN

1 ___ fin (6)
2 ___ factor (4-4)
3 ___ lamp (4)
4 ___ hamper (6)
5 ___ -friendly (4)
6 ___ advocate (6)
7 ___ -bearer (8)
10 ___ figures (6)
14 ___ stew (5)

16 ___ statesman (5)
17 ___ dancing (8)
18 ___ -breaker (6)
19 ___ virus (8)
21 ___ forces (6)
22 ___ collection (6)
24 ___ salad (6)
26 ___ leave (4)
28 ___ tea (4)

★★★★  123

Fill each blank square in the grid with the number 1, 2 or 3 so that each completed row and column has an equal number of 1s, 2s and 3s. Each bold rectangular block must contain all three numbers, and no two horizontally or vertically adjacent squares may contain the same number.

	2							
			3					2
			2					
		2					1	

SUDOKU SUM

Write a digit from 0-9 in each of the five blank spaces to make a calculation that works. No digit may be repeated in the sum.

```
    _  4  _
 +  3  _  2
 ----------
    _  _  9
```

★★★ Hitori

Black out certain squares in the grid so that no digit appears more than once in any row or column. Blacked-out squares may not touch each other horizontally or vertically, and all remaining squares must form a single continuous area.

5	6	1	6	3	2
2	1	2	5	2	3
6	6	2	1	4	5
1	5	2	2	2	4
5	2	4	1	1	6
2	3	5	6	2	3

OPPOSITE ATTRACTION

Unscramble the letters in the phrase HATE CYCLOPS to form two words that are opposites of each other.

_____   _____

★★★★ Codeword

Can you crack the code and complete the grid? Each letter of the alphabet appears at least once in the grid, and is represented by the same number throughout. The letter we've decoded should help you to identify other letters and words in the grid. If you would like a second and even a third starter letter, turn to page 255.

1		1		23		18		13		1		2		1
24	6	14	9	3	2	21	6	14		24	15	14	3	2
3		26		8		16		6		6		25		8
1	10	21	15	15		20	6	3	19	12		2	11	6
9		14						8				23		
	21	15	16	3		7	14	15	15	21	15	11	1	14
3				9		21				16		11		4
23	14	1	24	11	10	14		2	6	8	7	10 K	15	14
15		14		21				21		22				6
14	16	13	11	6	1	8	16	20		12	11	15	10	
		3				16						8		23
5	11	2		4	3	22	14	6		20	6	3	17	14
8		14		18		14		3		18		8		6
19	3	15	19	14		1	21	7	7	14	1	1	11	6
14		12		2		2		12		14		14		12

A B C D E F G H I J K̸ L M N O P Q R S T U V W X Y Z

1	2	3	4	5	6	7	8	9	10 K	11	12	13
14	15	16	17	18	19	20	21	22	23	24	25	26

★ Wordsearch – 60s & 70s Bands

Find the 23 listed pop groups of the 1960s & 1970s that are hidden in the grid. They may read horizontally, vertically or diagonally, and either backwards or forwards.

Animals
Beatles
Byrds
Casuals
Cream
Dakotas
Doors
Dreamers
Drifters
Easybeats
Equals
Faces
Fortunes
Hawkwind
Hollies
Kinks
Pirates
Searchers
Seekers
Springfields
Supremes
Tremeloes
Troggs

R	F	Q	Q	J	E	F	B	C	E	K	I	N	K	S
S	L	A	U	S	A	C	O	K	R	S	R	O	O	D
S	S	X	D	P	O	B	X	R	B	E	I	N	R	S
K	G	T	A	R	I	V	E	K	T	H	A	I	A	E
J	G	D	N	I	W	K	W	A	H	U	F	M	C	M
M	O	Y	I	N	S	S	F	S	T	T	N	Y	T	E
Z	R	Z	M	G	T	R	E	M	E	L	O	E	S	R
P	T	T	A	F	Y	E	E	R	S	S	E	T	S	P
E	V	L	L	I	K	M	S	H	E	L	A	S	S	U
O	B	D	S	E	R	A	A	T	C	E	A	E	S	S
W	B	D	R	L	W	E	A	F	B	R	C	U	H	M
P	Y	S	N	D	M	R	S	Y	N	A	A	G	Q	Z
J	R	L	U	S	I	D	S	C	F	R	Q	E	U	E
U	D	C	A	P	D	A	K	O	T	A	S	L	S	G
I	S	W	H	S	E	I	L	L	O	H	X	P	V	G

CHOP AND CHANGE

Delete one letter from the word DERANGED and rearrange the rest to get a person of high rank.

_____

★★★★ Turn Maze

Entering at the bottom and exiting at the top, find the shortest path through the maze, following these rules: you must turn right on red squares, turn left on blue squares, go straight through yellow squares and avoid black squares. You do not have to go through all the coloured squares. Your path may cross and retrace itself, but you may not simply reverse your direction.

ALTER EGO

Solve the anagram contained in the bold capital letters of the clue to find the name of a celebrity. Do you know their real name?

ENDOW LOYAL comedy actor and director

★★★ Crossword

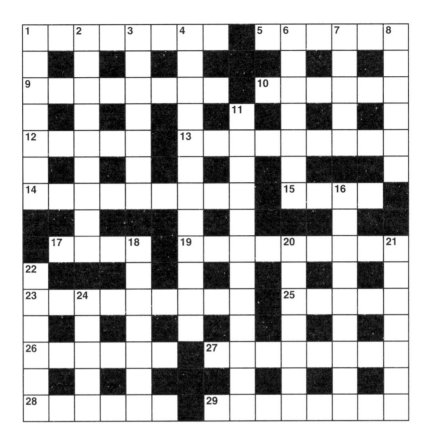

ACROSS

  1 Repudiate (8)
  5 Chopped (6)
  9 Of late (8)
 10 Make still (6)
 12 Effigy (5)
 13 Arguing logically (9)
 14 Monitor progress (4,5)
 15 Old Irish (4)
 17 Collar fastener (4)
 19 With intent to kill (9)
 23 Getting louder, musically (9)
 25 Piebald horse (5)
 26 Admit to holy orders (6)
 27 Dreamer (8)
 28 Albania's capital city (6)
 29 Tawny and streaked (8)

DOWN

  1 Drilling frame (7)
  2 Religious rite (9)
  3 Tolerant (7)
  4 Cruelty (3-9)
  6 Wondrous (7)
  7 Colour of army uniforms (5)
  8 Impair (6)
 11 Instruction to a financial institution (7,5)
 16 Tall, white wading bird (9)
 18 Clarity of speaking (7)
 20 Account for (7)
 21 Wore (7)
 22 Waylay (6)
 24 Church official (5)

★★★★ ABCD

Enter the letters A, B, C and D into the diagram so that each row and column has exactly one A, one B, one C and one D, leaving two blank boxes in each row and column. The letters outside the diagram indicate the first letter encountered, moving in the direction of the arrow.

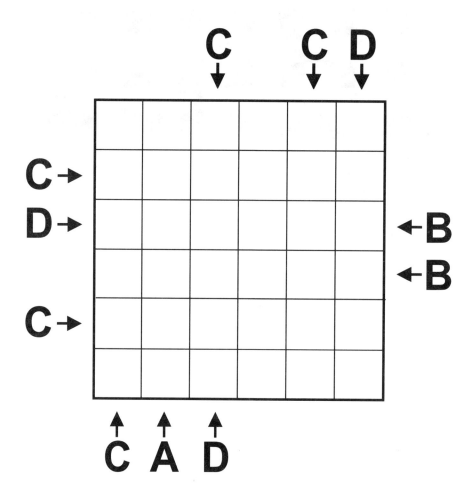

THREE OF A KIND

Find three hidden words in the sentence that, read in order, go together in some way.

Long ago in Great Britain, William of Orange was growing older

★★★★ Sudoku

Fill in all the empty cells in the grid so that each row, each column and each 3x3 block contains all the digits from 1-9.

				3	4			
	2					9		
			7	1			8	
		8						9
7		9		4		2		6
3						1		
	1			8	6			
		3					1	
			5	7				

BRAINSTRETCHER

Choose the lettered answer that best copies the pattern of the first link. Some lateral thinking is required.

perch is to *air*, as *jetty* is to:

(a) docks (b) water (c) wind current (d) fjord

★★★ Pieceword

Fit the blocks together in the empty grid to complete the crossword. Answers to the Across clues fit somewhere in the row with that number. The grid pattern follows central symmetry, that is, the top left corresponds to the bottom right, and the top right to the bottom left.

CENTRAL
SYMMETRY
PATTERN

ACROSS

1 Made safe • Common name for man's closest relative

3 Thin transparent fabric • Motorcycle attachment

5 Past its best (of fruit) • Pure

7 Hit back • Gnat or fly

9 Soldier's civilian dress • Imposing tomb

11 Brief pang • Pilfering

13 Indent with a mark • Airman, pilot

15 Faint • Tidied the feathers

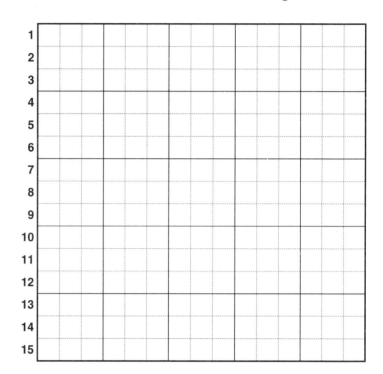

★★★★ One-Way Streets

The diagram represents a pattern of streets. P's are parking spaces, and the black squares are shops. Find the route that starts at a parking space, passes through all the shops exactly once, and ends at the other parking space. Arrows indicate one-way traffic for that block only. No block or intersection may be entered more than once.

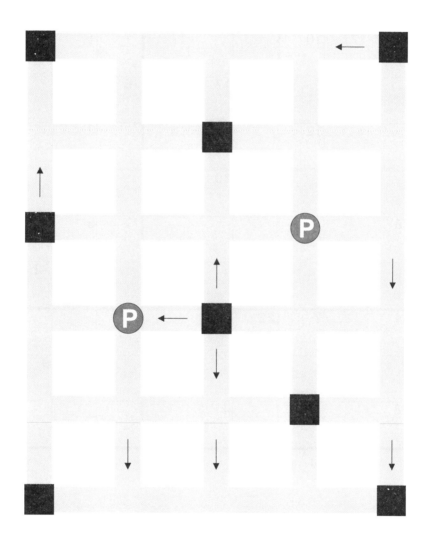

INITIAL REACTION

The words of a well-known proverb or saying have been reduced to their initial letters. Can you restore the missing words?

T N P L H _____

★★★★ Killer Sudoku

As in regular sudoku, fill all the empty cells in the grid so that each row, each column and each 3x3 block contains all the digits from 1-9. In addition, the digits in each dotted-line shape must add up to the number given in the top left corner of the shape, and no digit may be repeated within each dotted shape.

23	17	10			17		17	
1				17		15		
1	4	12			13		3	
1	7	15	10	20			19	
16						17	5	
1	12		10					22
11		7	22					
3					13			9
28				4		7		

CHOP AND CHANGE

Delete one letter from the word ARMISTICE and rearrange the rest to get a type of weapon.

_____

★★★★ Codeword

Can you crack the code and complete the grid? Each letter of the alphabet appears at least once in the grid, and is represented by the same number throughout. The letter we've decoded should help you to identify other letters and words in the grid. If you would like a second and even a third starter letter, turn to page 255.

21	26	16	20	23	26			13	3	7	23	14	17	5	
26		26		14		9		13		2		20		10	
23	6	11	26	6	9	19	26	11		13	3	10	2	26	
14		12		13		20		18		17		2		11	
23	9	20	7	11		23	20	7	17	21	17	26	23	23	
6		11				26		26		26				26	
	26	3	14	17	26	17	9	26		11	20	8	26	11	
24		26		26			7			26		26		25	
7	21	21	26	11		10	11	20	20	21	14	17	5		
17				8		26		21				6		1	
14	17	23	16	26	9	6	26	21		12	13	14	6	19	
16		16		2		1 W		14		11		2		26	
26	2	14	6	26		26	15	6	11	14	9	13	6	26	
11		11		23		26		4		13		6		22	
	16	26	11	23	20	17	13		10	11	26	26	22	26	

A B C D E F G H I J K L M N O P Q R S T U V ̷W X Y Z

1 W	2	3	4	5	6	7	8	9	10	11	12	13
14	15	16	17	18	19	20	21	22	23	24	25	26

★★★★ T-Rex Maze

Find the shortest path through the maze that passes through every red dot exactly once. You may not retrace your path.

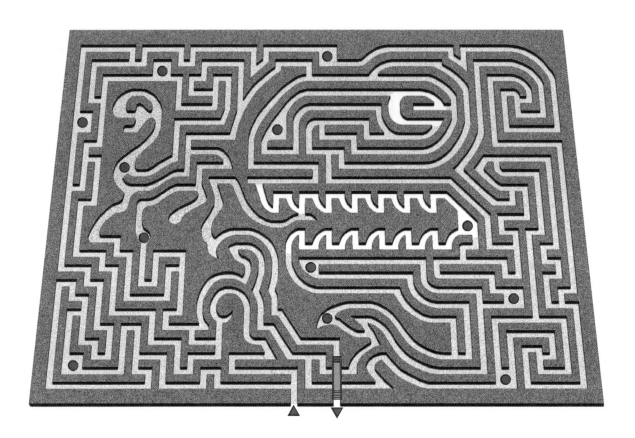

LOOK HEAR

Can you name and spell these 3 homophones (words that sound the same but have different meanings) from the definitions given?

solder at high temperature; cook slowly; cries like a donkey

★★★★ Star Search

Find the stars that are hidden in some of the blank squares. The numbered squares indicate how many stars are hidden in the squares adjacent to them (including diagonally). There is never more than one star in any square.

TELEPHONE TRIOS

Using the numbers and letters on the telephone keypad, what three seven-letter words, names or phrases on a common theme can be formed from the numbers below?

7822377 __ __ __ __ __ __ __

8748674 __ __ __ __ __ __ __

8428679 __ __ __ __ __ __ __

	ABC	DEF
1	**2**	**3**
GHI **4**	JKL **5**	MNO **6**
PRS **7**	TUV **8**	WXY **9**
✻	**0**	**#**

★★★ Jig-a-Link

With the help of the single starter letter, fit all the listed words into the grid.

3 letters
Ale
Cos
Eau
Ego
Ira
Lee
Nag
Nod

4 letters
Acid
Anti
Data
Earn
Ecru
Form
Gist
Halt
Hint
Ibis
Idol
Item
Keen
Sell
Stab
Thud

5 letters
Brief
Climb
Coral
Daisy
Dined
Domed
Ennui
Faced
Gleam
Grief
Hello
Hoist
Laden
Leapt
Leech
Liken
Mined
Offal
Shrew
Slump
Tight
Tilde
Tying
Vaunt

6 letters
Airily
Bathed
Beheld
Belted
Bodega
Cooled
Curacy
Deadly
Debtor
Felony
Having
Lowest
Mellow
Midget
Mouldy
Mugged
Panted
Really
Salted
Tawdry
Tether
Tragic
Wilder
Yearly

★★★ Hitori

Black out certain squares in the grid so that no digit appears more than once in any row or column. Blacked-out squares may not touch each other horizontally or vertically, and all remaining squares must form a single continuous area.

5	2	3	6	1	2
6	2	3	1	4	4
1	5	2	2	6	1
3	2	5	2	4	6
1	6	5	4	5	5
4	4	1	5	3	5

OPPOSITE ATTRACTION

Unscramble the letters in the phrase PIANO RENTAL to form two words that are opposites of each other.

_____   _____

★★★ Line Drawing

Draw two straight lines, each from one edge of the square to another edge, to create three regions, each one containing the same number of circles.

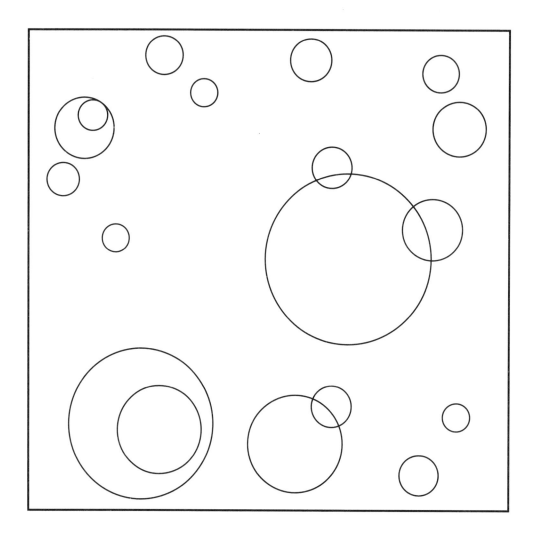

BETWEENER

What six-letter word can be inserted between the two words below to make a well-known expression with each?

RED __ __ __ __ __ __ CLEANER

★★★ Crossword

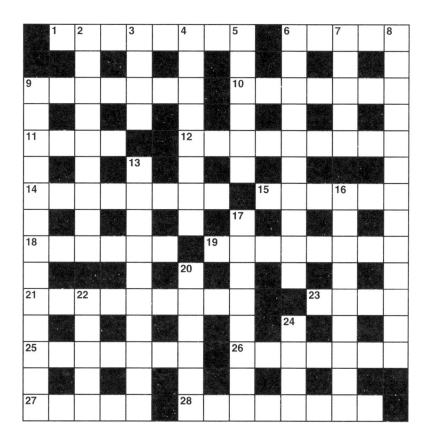

ACROSS

1 Kidnapped (8)

6 Provisional certificate of money (5)

9 Ceremonial garb (7)

10 Pernicious (7)

11 Name linking Montand and Saint Laurent (4)

12 Containing compressed air (9)

14 Damaged (of certain fabrics) (8)

15 Leafy bower (6)

18 Moored (of a ship) (2,4)

19 Philosophy maintaining that existence is without objective meaning or purpose (8)

21 Emergency evacuation practice (4,5)

23 Fillip (4)

25 Legendary twin suckled by a wolf (7)

26 American car make (7)

27 Greek Muse of love poetry (5)

28 Alienate (8)

DOWN

2 Conceited (3-6)

3 Citrus fruit hybrid (4)

4 Walked wearily (8)

5 1960s Czech leader (6)

6 Bird known as a bank swallow in the US (4,6)

7 Ship's modernisation (5)

8 Multicoloured (13)

9 Branch of the British armed forces (5,3,5)

13 Minor sin (10)

16 Undergoing a reaction in which electrons are lost (9)

17 Swift's land of tiny people (8)

20 Mass of cells (6)

22 Latin-American dance (5)

24 Ancient South American (4)

★★ Triad Split Decisions

In this crossword without clues, each answer consists of two words that share common letters, but diverge into different words through the consecutive letters given. All answers are common words; no proper nouns (names), phrases or hyphenated words are used. More than one word pair may fit a particular section of the grid, but only one of the pairs will correctly link up with all the other word pairs.

CHOP AND CHANGE

Delete one letter from the word **INTROSPECTIVE** and rearrange the rest to get an office job.

_____

HINTS AND TIPS ON SOLVING PUZZLES

Answers to all the puzzles are given, beginning on page 230. They are organised by the page number on which each puzzle appears.

WORD PUZZLES

CROSSWORD

This puzzle needs little introduction. We've included straight crosswords, as well as some of the many variations, such as All in One, Anagram and Cryptic. Also featured are crosswords with non-standard grids, such as Honeycomb, Roundabout, Continuity and Look Both Ways. All the solving instructions you'll need for these puzzles are given on the page.

Hint: Even the most straightforward crosswords may stump you with a particular clue or awkward section. If you're stuck for an answer, try entering probable letters in the grid, such as -ED, -ING or -S endings, which may help with intersecting answers.

PIECEWORD

The task here is to re-create a crossword in an empty grid, using the 3x3 answer blocks, plus clues to some of the answers.

Hints: Look for a row of clues that seems likely to fill the whole row. Once you've spotted the correct blocks to make the answers, positioning them will be easy. Pay attention to the grid's symmetry, which will narrow your choice of blocks as the puzzle progresses.

SKELETON CROSSWORD

This is a crossword with an added twist. You must work out the grid pattern as you go along, filling in the black squares as well as the answers.

Hints: Don't be intimidated by the lack of a grid. A careful setter will have given plenty of clues to the grid pattern in the starter numbers and squares. Don't forget that any square to the left of an Across clue number must be black, as is any square above a Down clue number. Once you have marked these squares in the grid, don't forget to enter their symmetrical counterparts. Check the list of clues for numbers that are shared by both Across and Down clues: the fact that these answers have a first letter in common may help you to solve them.

CLUELESS CROSSWORD

Complete the crossword with common seven-letter words, working from the letters already filled in for you.

EXAMPLE   SOLUTION

Hints: Focusing on the endings of words often helps. For example, a last letter of G often suggests that IN are the previous two letters. Focus on the shared blank spaces – you can often figure out whether a letter must be a vowel or a consonant, helping you to solve both words that cross it.

SPLIT DECISIONS

The only clues to these crosswords are within the grid. Each answer consists of two words that share common letters, but diverge into different words through the consecutive letters given. All answers are common words; no proper nouns, phrases or hyphenated words are used. More than one word pair may fit a particular section of the grid, but only one of the pairs will link up with all the others.

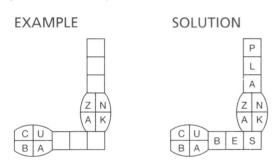

EXAMPLE   SOLUTION

Hints: Start with the shorter words, because there will be fewer word possibilities. In each puzzle, there will be some word pairs that have only one solution. Look also for uncommon letters such as Q, Z and J. These may lead to an obvious word.

CODEWORD

In this puzzle you must crack the code and complete the grid. A codeword is a completed crossword grid in which each letter of the alphabet has been substituted

for a number from 1 to 26. There will be at least one occurrence of each letter of the alphabet, and the letter will be represented by the same number, wherever it appears in the grid. Three letters are usually decoded to get you started. Write these letters in wherever their numbers appear in the grid, and you should then have enough clues to start identifying other letters and words in the grid. All answers are common words; no phrases, hyphenated words or proper nouns are used.

Hints: If you can't immediately guess any full words from the letters in the grid, look for common letter combinations, such as -NESS, -ING and -ED endings. Repeated letters, such as AN in BANANA, often yield useful clues. Be sure to use the reference grid and letter list below the puzzle to keep track of the letters you have (and more importantly haven't) used.

LOGIC PUZZLES

SUDOKU

Sudoku puzzles have become hugely popular in recent years, thanks to their simplicity as a test of pure reasoning. The basic sudoku puzzle is a 9x9 square grid, split into 9 square blocks, each containing 9 cells. Each puzzle starts off with roughly 20 to 35 of the cells filled in with any of the numbers 1 to 9. There is just one rule: the rest of the cells must be filled in with the missing numbers from 1 to 9 so that no number appears twice in any row, column or 3x3 block.

EXAMPLE   SOLUTION

Hints: Use the numbers provided to eliminate places where the same number can't appear. For example, if there is already 1 in a cell, then 1 cannot appear again in that same row, column or 3x3 block. By scanning all the cells that the various 1s rule out, often you can find where missing 1s must go.

HYPER-SUDOKU

This variation of sudoku is solved in much the same way as the original. In addition to the numbers 1 to 9 appearing in each row and column and each of the nine 3x3 blocks marked with bold lines, hyper-sudoku has four more 3x3 blocks to work with. These are marked with grey shading.

EXAMPLE   SOLUTION

KILLER SUDOKU

This puzzle uses the solving skills of sudoku, but in addition the digits within each dotted-line shape imposed on top of the

sudoku grid must add up to the number in the top left corner of each shape. No digit may be repeated within a dotted-line shape.

EXAMPLE

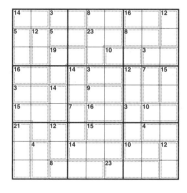

SOLUTION

Hints: Look for unique digit answers in the dotted-line shapes. For example, two squares totalling 17 must contain a 9 and an 8. Two squares totalling 4 must contain a 1 and a 3, as two 2s would not be allowed. Don't get so involved in the totals that you forget to use normal sudoku solving methods as well.

123

EXAMPLE   SOLUTION

Each grid in this puzzle has bold rectangular blocks that look like dominoes. You must fill in the blank squares so that each 'domino' contains one each of the numbers 1, 2 and 3, according to these two rules:

1 No two adjacent squares, horizontally or vertically, can have the same number.
2 Each completed row and column of the diagram will have an equal number of 1s, 2s and 3s.

Hints: Look first for any blank square that is adjacent to two different numbers. By rule 1 above, the 'missing' number from 1, 2 and 3 must go in that blank square. Rule 2 becomes important to use later in the solving process. Knowing that, for example, a 9-by-9 diagram must have three 1s, three 2s and three 3s in each row and column allows you to use the process of elimination to deduce what blank squares in nearly filled rows and columns must contain.

FIND THE SHIPS

You'll find a step-by-step solving guide to this puzzle in the masterclass on pages 4-5.

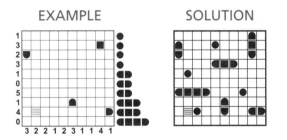

EXAMPLE   SOLUTION

In each puzzle, a group of ships is listed on the right. Your job is to place the ships in the grid. A handful of ship 'parts' are positioned to get you started. The placement rules are:
1 Ships must be oriented horizontally or vertically. No diagonals!
2 A square with wavy lines indicates water and will not contain part of a ship.

3 The numbers at the edge of the grid indicate how many squares in that row or column contain parts of ships.
4 No two ships can touch each other, not even diagonally.

Hints: You can eliminate all squares in a row or column that is marked with a 0 outside the grid. If you know that a square will be occupied by part of a ship, but don't yet know the type of ship, mark the square and eliminate all squares that are diagonally adjacent to it.

ABC

Each row and column in an ABC puzzle contains exactly one A, one B and one C, plus one blank square (or two, in harder puzzles). Your task is to figure out where the three letters go in each row. The clues outside the puzzle frame tell you the first letter encountered when moving in the direction of the arrow.

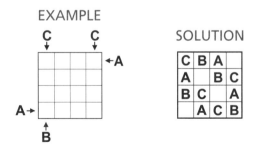

EXAMPLE   SOLUTION

Hints: If a clue says a letter is first in a row or column, don't assume that it must go in the first square. It could go in either of the first two squares (or any of the first three, in the harder puzzles). A good way to start is to look for places where row and column clues intersect (especially where they point directly towards the same square). These clues often give you the most information about where the first letter of a row or column must go.

FENCES

Connect adjacent dots with vertical or horizontal lines, so that a single loop with no crossings or branches is formed in the grid. Each number indicates how many lines surround it. Square spaces with no number may be surrounded by any number of lines.

EXAMPLE   SOLUTION

Hints: Don't try to solve the puzzle by making one continuous line – instead, connect any dots you can, then figure out how to connect those links. To start, mark any links that can't be connected, ie all four links around each 0. Where a 3 is adjacent to a 0, the route of the three small lines is clear.

HITORI

Black out certain squares in the grid so that no digit appears more than once in any row or column. Blacked-out squares may not touch each other horizontally or vertically, and all remaining squares must form a single continuous area.

EXAMPLE   SOLUTION

5	3	1	4	3
4	5	3	4	2
2	1	2	3	4
1	3	2	1	4
3	4	2	5	4

Hints: Circle any digits that appear only once in their row and column, as their squares will never be shaded. Since blacked-out squares may not touch each other horizontally or vertically, any square that sits directly between a pair of the same digits must remain unshaded, no matter what its digit is. Once a square is shaded, you know that the squares horizontally and vertically adjacent to it will be unshaded.

STAR SEARCH

Find the stars that are hidden in some of the blank squares. The numbered squares indicate how many stars are hidden in the squares adjacent to them (including diagonally). There is never more than one star in any square.

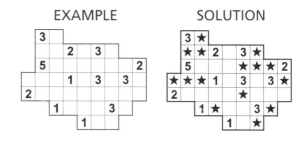

EXAMPLE   SOLUTION

Hint: If, for example, a 3 is surrounded by four empty squares, but two of those squares are adjacent to the same square containing a 1, the other two empty squares around the 3 must contain stars.

FITWORD & JIG-A-LINK

Though they look like word puzzles, these really have more in common with logic puzzles. Essentially the puzzle is a jigsaw in which the pieces are words to be correctly positioned in a crossword grid. You will have to think one or two steps ahead in this puzzle, to work out which of the possible words for a space will fit with all of its neighbours.

Hint: Keep looking around the grid. If the section you've reached seems to have too many options to narrow down, there's likely to be an easier step elsewhere.

NUMBER JIG

This works on exactly the same principle as fitword and jig-a-link, but with numbers rather than words.

Hints: The fitword hint holds true for this puzzle too. Move around the grid. It's often easiest to concentrate at first on the sections of the listed numbers that have fewest entries, so you have fewer possible numbers to eliminate for a particular space in the grid. Don't forget to enter all the information you can in the grid. Even if you can't tell which of two numbers fits a space, there may be digits in the same position in both numbers that you can write in the grid, giving clues to intersecting numbers.

VISUAL PUZZLES

Throughout *Mind Stretchers* you will find unique mazes, visual conundrums and other colourful challenges. Each comes under a new name and has unique instructions. Our best advice? Be patient and persevere. You will need time to unravel the visual secrets. In addition, you will find examples of the following visual challenges.

LINE DRAWINGS

Each line drawing puzzle is different in its design, but the task is the same: figure out where to place the prescribed number of lines to partition the space as directed.

Hint: Use a pencil and ruler. Some lines come very close to the items within the region, so being straight and accurate with your line-drawing is crucial.

ONE-WAY STREETS

The diagram represents a pattern of streets. A and B are parking spaces, and the black squares are shops. Find a route that starts at A, passes through all the shops exactly once, and ends at B. Arrows indicate one-way traffic for that block only. No block or intersection may be entered more than once. P's replace A and B in some harder puzzles.

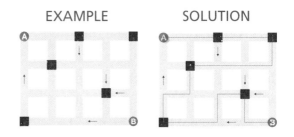

EXAMPLE   SOLUTION

Hints: The particular arrangement of shops and arrows will always limit the possibilities for the first shop visited from the starting point A and the last shop visited before reaching B. So try to work both from the start and the end of the route. Also, the placement of an arrow on a block doesn't necessarily mean that your route will pass through that block.

WORDSEARCH

In this enduring favourite, the challenge is to find hidden words within a grid of letters. In a typical puzzle, words can be found in vertical columns, horizontal rows and along diagonals, with the letters of the words running either forwards or backwards. Usually, a list of words to search for is given. To make wordsearches harder, puzzle setters sometimes just point you in the right direction, such as telling you to find 25 foods.

Hints: One of the most reliable and efficient searching methods is to scan each row from top to bottom for the first letter of the word. If the puzzle has no list, the most efficient solving strategy is to scan the rows, columns and diagonals methodically for words.

PATHFINDER

The task in this puzzle is to find a path of words through the grid. The first letter or step is usually highlighted. The trail then twists up, down, left or right, one letter at a time (never diagonally) through every letter of the grid. To make things slightly harder, we may not list the items to be found on the trail. If not, we will point you in the right direction, with a description of the category of items to be found, and the number that appear.

EXAMPLE

```
S  P  D  T  R  I  A  N  G
E  H  I  M  Y  P  A  T  L
S  E  R  A  R  E  G  N  E
P  I  E  C  O  N  O  E  P
L  L  R  H  B  U  N  X  A
E  E  L  O  M  S  H  E  G
I  R  C  R  E  D  N  I  O
C  G  N  R  E  C  Y  L  N
E  L  A  T  C  L  A  V  O
```

SOLUTION

Hint: Pencil is advisable for this puzzle. Occasionally you may take a plausible direction in the puzzle which you then discover will not allow you to use every letter of the grid.

BRAINTEASERS

To complement the more involved puzzles are more than 100 short brainteasers, including word, number and logical puzzles. Each puzzle has its own instructions.

QUICK BRAINTEASERS

You'll also find quick brainteasers at the top of the right-hand pages in this book. There are three categories:

• Do You Know? These questions will test your knowledge of facts and trivia.

• True or False? Separate fact from fiction in this miscellany of numerical, factual and word-based teasers.

• What Word Links? Find a word that can precede or follow each of the three clue words to make a well-known expression.

The answers to the quick brainteasers are listed on pages 230-231, separate from the main puzzle answers.

ANSWERS

PAGE 7
Do You Know?
URUGUAY (1930)

PAGE 9
What Word Links?
PRINCE

PAGE 11
True or False?
TRUE – it is an oriental
tobacco pipe

PAGE 13
Do You Know?
HISPANIOLA

PAGE 15
What Word Links?
POWDER

PAGE 17
True or False?
TRUE

PAGE 19
Do You Know?
MARSEILLES

PAGE 21
What Word Links?
PART

PAGE 23
True or False?
TRUE

PAGE 25
Do You Know?
PETER BENCHLEY

PAGE 27
What Word Links?
WHEEL

PAGE 29
True or False?
FALSE – it should be
12345 + 44444

PAGE 31
Do You Know?
ASH WEDNESDAY

PAGE 33
What Word Links?
STAMP

PAGE 35
True or False?
TRUE – it is a small gull

PAGE 37
Do You Know?
ABBA (singing *Waterloo*)

PAGE 39
What Word Links?
CUP

PAGE 41
True or False?
TRUE – his fighting name
was Big Daddy

PAGE 43
Do You Know?
ALUMINIUM

PAGE 45
What Word Links?
DOG

PAGE 47
True or False?
FALSE – it is 25

PAGE 49
Do You Know?
PATRICK SWAYZE

PAGE 51
What Word Links?
BAG

PAGE 53
True or False?
TRUE (nectar was the
drink of the gods)

PAGE 55
Do You Know?
1837

PAGE 57
What Word Links?
CARD

PAGE 59
True or False?
FALSE – it measures
rainfall

PAGE 61
Do You Know?
THOMAS HUGHES

PAGE 63
What Word Links?
CHAIR

PAGE 65
True or False?
TRUE

PAGE 67
Do You Know?
AUSTRALIA

PAGE 69
What Word Links?
WISE

PAGE 71
True or False?
FALSE – it is 768 (32 teeth
x 24 ribs)

PAGE 73
Do You Know?
SUNFLOWER

PAGE 75
What Word Links?
TEA

PAGE 77
True or False?
FALSE – it is the botanical
name for the carnation

PAGE 79
Do You Know?
GUSTAV

PAGE 81
What Word Links?
HORN

PAGE 83
True or False?
TRUE – it commemorates
the end of World War II in
Europe

PAGE 85
Do You Know?
JOHN DUNLOP

PAGE 87
What Word Links?
BED

PAGE 89
True or False?
TRUE – it is 196, as
opposed to 216

PAGE 91
Do You Know?
A TYPE OF HORSE

PAGE 93
What Word Links?
CROSS

PAGE 95
True or False?
FALSE – she wrote *Gone
with the Wind*

PAGE 97
Do You Know?
MOTOR SPORT – it is
the home of the Belgian
Grand Prix

PAGE 99
What Word Links?
MOON

PAGE 101
True or False?
TRUE – it was the cart that
transported them to the
guillotine

PAGE 103
Do You Know?
GERMAN MEASLES

PAGE 105
What Word Links?
EYE

PAGE 107
True or False?
TRUE – it is a type of
greatcoat

PAGE 109
Do You Know?
POTATOES AND CABBAGE

PAGE 111
What Word Links?
AIR

PAGE 113
True or False?
FALSE – it describes
stormy areas of ocean in
the southern hemisphere,
between latitudes 40°
and 50°

PAGE 115
Do You Know?
FRANCE – it is a daily
newspaper

PAGE 117
What Word Links?
RACE

PAGE 119
True or False?
TRUE

PAGE 121
Do You Know?
EAT IT – it is a variety of cheese

PAGE 123
What Word Links?
SAFE

PAGE 125
True or False?
FALSE – it is 6 under par in golf (birdie, eagle and albatross are 1, 2 and 3 shots under par, respectively)

PAGE 127
Do You Know?
WALES – west of Swansea

PAGE 129
What Word Links?
FRONT

PAGE 131
True or False?
FALSE – it began on 1st January 2001

PAGE 133
Do You Know?
J K ROWLING

PAGE 135
What Word Links?
GLASS

PAGE 137
True or False?
FALSE – he was their friend

PAGE 139
Do You Know?
GIACOMO PUCCINI

PAGE 141
What Word Links?
WASH

PAGE 143
True or False?
FALSE – it is 8000

PAGE 145
Do You Know?
MALI

PAGE 147
What Word Links?
IRON

PAGE 149
True or False?
TRUE

PAGE 151
Do You Know?
24

PAGE 153
What Word Links?
WATCH

PAGE 155
True or False?
FALSE – it is a strong tobacco from Louisiana

PAGE 157
Do You Know?
Na

PAGE 159
What Word Links?
NEWS

PAGE 161
True or False?
TRUE

PAGE 163
Do You Know?
LORD LOUIS MOUNTBATTEN

PAGE 165
What Word Links?
COAT

PAGE 167
True or False?
TRUE – it is egg white

PAGE 169
Do You Know?
RON MOODY

PAGE 171
What Word Links?
CIRCLE

PAGE 173
True or False?
TRUE – it is native to Indonesia, also known as a flying fox

PAGE 175
Do You Know?
KATIE PRICE

PAGE 177
What Word Links?
RAIN

PAGE 179
True or False?
TRUE – it was also once called Constantinople

PAGE 181
Do You Know?
TOMMY COOPER

PAGE 183
What Word Links?
STAR

PAGE 185
True or False?
FALSE – it is the study of flags

PAGE 187
Do You Know?
LEWES

PAGE 189
What Word Links?
BLOCK

PAGE 191
True or False?
FALSE – it is a small fort or earthwork, or a candle holder

PAGE 193
Do You Know?
ELECTRIC LIGHT SWITCHES

PAGE 195
True or False?
TRUE

PAGE 197
What Word Links?
MOUSE

PAGE 199
True or False?
TRUE – Alexandre Dumas, père

PAGE 201
Do You Know?
EUCALYPTUS SHOOTS

PAGE 203
What Word Links?
STOCK

PAGE 205
True or False?
FALSE – it is now called Chennai; Bombay is now Mumbai

PAGE 207
Do You Know?
THE RED CRESCENT

PAGE 209
What Word Links?
COUNTRY

PAGE 211
True or False?
TRUE – but only when considered as a sum of their atomic numbers: oxygen (8) + helium (2) = neon (10)

PAGE 213
Do You Know?
BOCCACCIO

PAGE 215
What Word Links?
SPELL

PAGE 217
True or False?
TRUE – it is a fish

PAGE 219
Do You Know?
FLOWERS IN THE RAIN
(by The Move)

232

PAGE 6

Find the Ships

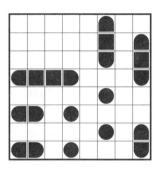

BETWEENER
PAINT

PAGE 7

Codeword

PAGE 8

Four Square

AND SO ON
SOAP and WATER

PAGE 9

Wordsearch – The Big Cheese

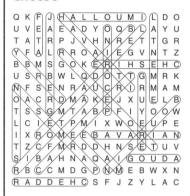

INITIAL REACTION
Look Before You Leap

PAGE 10

Sudoku

3	1	9	2	8	4	7	6	5
5	8	6	9	1	7	3	4	2
2	4	7	5	3	6	9	8	1
4	3	2	7	5	8	6	1	9
8	7	1	6	9	2	4	5	3
6	9	5	3	4	1	2	7	8
7	5	4	1	2	9	8	3	6
1	2	8	4	6	3	5	9	7
9	6	3	8	7	5	1	2	4

MAKE TRACKS
1 Solar 2 Jelly 3 Drift 4 Snoop
5 Steed. POMEGRANATE and
CAULIFLOWER

PAGE 11

Crossword

PAGE 12

Fences

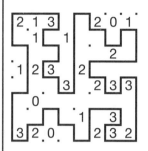

ADDITION SWITCH
128 + 506 = 634

PAGE 13

Line Drawing

HEN, ARIA, STATUE, EERIE

ALTER EGO
JULIE ANDREWS (Julie Wells)

PAGE 14

Wordsearch - Castles

BRAINSTRETCHER
SUPPORT. Underscore and stress
are synonymous, as are underpin
and support

PAGE 15
Number Jig

```
2 0 8 0 3 | 1 |   1 2 3 9 |   2
2 |   8 |   3 |   8 2 0 |   2 0 4 2
9 5 0 4 4 5 |   1 4 3 0 |   6
4 |   6 |   3 |   3 |   3 |   1 |   4 1 7
9 7 8 7 4 1 |   6 |   6 6 6 3 4
6 |   8 |   3 3 4 1 |   7 |   5 |   5
6 2 6 5 4 2 |   2 |   4 7 8 7 0 2
  6 |   9 1 2 6 1 |   5
8 8 5 7 5 6 |   4 |   6 5 7 7 3 6
7 |   8 |   5 |   9 8 3 4 |   7 |   2
3 3 4 3 2 |   4 |   7 2 3 7 0 0
1 0 1 |   8 |   6 |   1 |   1 7 0
  7 |   8 7 6 5 |   9 3 0 2 5 8 0
4 5 5 1 |   9 7 5 |   7 |   7 |   4
  8 |   6 0 4 7 |   6 |   5 4 4 0 4
```

PAGE 16
Codeword

```
R E H E A T █ E P I C █ S U M
I █ A █ M █ S █ R █ A █ U █ A
C O M M I T T E E █ L O B B Y
H █ M █ S █ R █ S █ C █ J █ B
█ B O N S A I █ S Q U E E Z E
C █ C █ D █ L █ C █ █ L █ C
H I K E D █ E X T R A C T E D
A █ E █ N █ A █ T █ █ U █ A
P A R A S I T I C █ E X P E L
█ A █ E █ T █ L █ L █ Y █ █
W H I R R E D █ L A R G E R █
H █ L █ T █ R █ E █ U █ N █ S
A L I B I █ O B S E R V A N T
L █ N █ O █ W █ S █ A █ R █ U
E G G █ N O N E █ F L A Y E D
```

```
L I V R G H N P T X Z O D
U S J M Y K Q C F E W A B
```

PAGE 17
Killer Sudoku

```
7 5 2 4 8 6 9 1 3
3 4 8 9 2 1 7 5 6
6 9 1 5 7 3 4 8 2
1 6 5 3 4 7 8 2 9
2 7 9 8 1 5 3 6 4
8 3 4 2 6 9 5 7 1
4 2 6 7 3 8 1 9 5
5 8 3 1 9 2 6 4 7
9 1 7 6 5 4 2 3 8
```

RHYMING TRIO
MAC, TACK, WHACK

PAGE 18
Skeleton Crossword

```
O U T W A R D █ G A S T R I C
C █ I █ I █ E V E █ A █ A █ R
T U T O R █ P █ N █ U N D U E
O █ L █ E D I T I O N █ I █ A
B L E E D █ C █ A █ A B O U T
E █ █ Y █ S T I L L █ U █ O
R E G E N T █ N █ U N F A I R
█ M █ S █ R U L E R █ F █ R
A U R O R A █ E █ C O A T E D
S █ R █ P I T C H █ L █ U
H A R E M █ N █ Y █ T O K E N
A █ O █ A M M O N I A █ N █ G
M O O D Y █ A █ I █ P R I C E
E █ T █ O █ T I C █ E █ F █ O
D E S E R V E █ S U R G E O N
```

PAGE 19
One-Way Streets

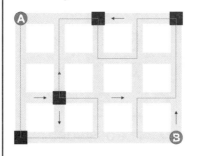

LOGICAL
The motorbike finished first and travelled by A-roads.
1st, motorbike, A-roads
2nd, car, B-roads
3rd, van, motorways

PAGE 20
Out of Order

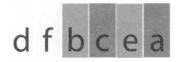

CHOP AND CHANGE
BLOUSE (drop the D)

PAGE 21
Star Search

TELEPHONE TRIOS
EL GRECO, PICASSO, VAN GOGH

PAGE 22
Killer Sudoku

```
3 2 8 5 9 1 4 6 7
6 7 4 3 2 8 9 1 5
1 9 5 4 6 7 2 8 3
5 6 9 8 3 4 1 7 2
4 1 3 2 7 9 8 5 6
2 8 7 1 5 6 3 4 9
7 4 2 6 8 3 5 9 1
9 3 1 7 4 5 6 2 8
8 5 6 9 1 2 7 3 4
```

INITIAL REACTION
He Who Hesitates Is Lost

PAGE 23
Crossword

```
P L U M █ H I T C H H I K E D
L █ N █ S █ N █ O █ A █ O █ R
Y E N T L █ M A K E M E R R Y
M █ A █ E █ O █ E █ M █ E █ R
O P T E D O U T █ D E J A V U
U █ U █ G █ R █ G █ R █ █ N
T I R E E █ N E A R S I D E █
H █ A █ █ I █ M █ █ R █ G
█ E L E G A N C E █ A M I G O
G █ █ E █ G █ K █ M █ F █ L
A B O A R D █ R E V O L T E D
U █ M █ M █ E █ U █ W █ M
C O C K A H O O P █ N A O M I
H █ U █ N █ T █ E █ T █ O █ N
E V E R Y W H E R E █ E D G E
```

PAGE 24

Hyper-Sudoku

4	1	8	3	9	6	7	5	2
3	2	5	4	7	8	6	1	9
6	9	7	1	2	5	3	4	8
1	6	3	8	5	2	9	7	4
7	5	4	6	1	9	2	8	3
9	8	2	7	3	4	5	6	1
5	3	1	9	4	7	8	2	6
2	4	6	5	8	3	1	9	7
8	7	9	2	6	1	4	3	5

AND SO ON
STICKS and STONES

PAGE 25

Child's Play

Picture 4

BETWEENER
AIR

PAGE 26

123

1	2	1	3	2	3
2	1	3	2	3	1
3	2	1	3	1	2
1	3	2	1	2	3
3	1	3	2	1	2
2	3	2	1	3	1

SUDOKU SUM
109 + 247 = 356

PAGE 27

Codeword

PAGE 28

ABC

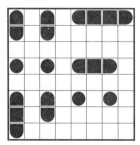

CLUELESS CROSSWORD

J	U	I	C	E	R	S
E		N		X		A
A	W	K	W	A	R	D
L		L		M		D
O	X	I	D	I	S	E
U		N		N		S
S	E	G	M	E	N	T

PAGE 29

Find the Ships

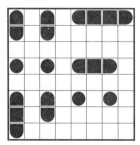

ALTER EGO
W C FIELDS
(William Claude Dukenfield)

PAGE 30

Wordsearch – Film Genres

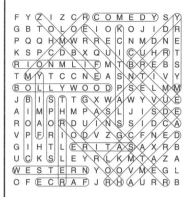

INITIAL REACTION
WASTE NOT, WANT NOT

PAGE 31

Skeleton Crossword

PAGE 32

Koala Maze

RHYMING TRIO
PEA, SKI, THREE

Fences

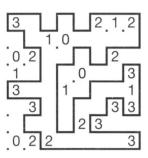

ADDITION SWITCH
184 + 379 = 563

Killer Sudoku

4	1	9	3	5	7	8	6	2
8	3	7	6	9	2	1	4	5
2	5	6	8	4	1	3	7	9
6	4	8	1	7	5	9	2	3
7	9	1	2	3	4	6	5	8
3	2	5	9	6	8	4	1	7
9	8	2	7	1	6	5	3	4
5	6	3	4	2	9	7	8	1
1	7	4	5	8	3	2	9	6

AND SO ON
BEER and SKITTLES

Crossword

O	U	T	C	O	M	E	■	A	G	A	I	N	S	T
N	■	A	■	I	■	T	■	O	■	G	■	T		
S	C	A	R	■	A	L	O	O	F	■	L	E	A	D
A	■	R	■	M	■	P	■	O	■	O	■	M		
I	N	V	I	T	I	N	G	■	R	O	O	K	I	E
N	■	E	■	U	■	W	■	■	N	■	■	N		
D	Y	E	D	■	P	A	N	C	A	K	E	D	A	Y
■	O	■	L	■	R	■	X							
T	H	I	N	K	A	L	O	U	D	■	C	I	T	Y
A	■	S	■	R	■	L	■	R						
S	T	U	A	R	T	■	C	U	L	T	U	R	A	L
C	■	D	■	E	■	H	■	A	■	S	■	D		
W	H	I	M	■	R	E	I	G	N	■	I	V	E	S
E	■	I	■	E	■	D	■	Z	■	O	■	I		
S	T	A	T	U	R	E	■	W	A	R	N	I	N	G

Sudoku

2	1	9	3	6	4	8	7	5
8	7	3	5	9	1	2	6	4
4	6	5	8	7	2	1	3	9
5	4	1	9	8	6	7	2	3
7	2	8	1	4	3	5	9	6
3	9	6	7	2	5	4	8	1
6	5	4	2	3	7	9	1	8
1	8	2	6	5	9	3	4	7
9	3	7	4	1	8	6	5	2

BRAINSTRETCHER
PISCES. The star sign Pisces follows Aquarius, as Virgo follows Leo

123

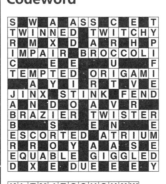

SUDOKU SUM
218 + 439 = 657

Codeword

S	■	W	■	A	■	A	S	S	■	C	■	E	■	T
T	W	I	N	N	E	D	■	T	W	I	T	C	H	Y
R	■	M	■	X	■	D	■	A	■	R	■	H	■	P
I	M	P	A	I	R	■	B	R	O	C	C	O	L	I
C	■	■	E	■	E	■	■	U	■	■	U	■	■	F
T	E	M	P	T	E	D	■	O	R	I	G	A	M	I
■	A	■	Y	■	I	■	R	■	T	■	V	■	E	
J	I	N	X	■	S	T	I	N	K	■	F	E	N	D
A	■	N	■	D	■	O	■	A	■	V	■	R		
B	R	A	Z	I	E	R	■	T	W	I	S	T	E	R
B	■	■	S	■	■	E	■	N	■	■	E			
E	S	C	O	R	T	E	D	■	A	T	R	I	U	M
R	■	R	■	O	■	Y	■	A	■	A	■	S	■	E
E	Q	U	A	B	L	E	■	G	I	G	G	L	E	D
D	■	X	■	E	■	D	U	E	■	E	■	E	■	Y

| K | L | T | M | J | Z | O | S | H | Q | U | X | W |
| N | R | Y | B | A | G | F | V | E | C | I | D | P |

One-Way Streets

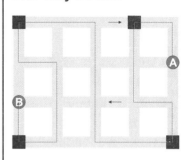

TAKE TWO
DRAGON

Sequence Maze

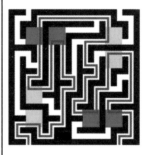

MAKE TRACKS
1 Mouth 2 Peace 3 Globe
4 Enrol 5 Deter. MONEYLENDER and STOCKBROKER

Star Search

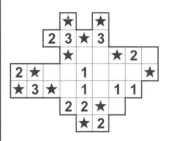

TELEPHONE TRIOS
BROTHER, GRANDPA, HUSBAND

PAGE 42

Pieceword

PAGE 43

Wordsearch – Islands

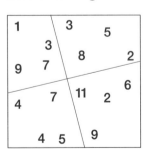

CHOP AND CHANGE
INQUEST (drop the A)

PAGE 45

Line Drawing

THREE OF A KIND
OVER THE TOP

PAGE 46

ABC

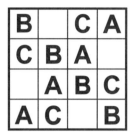

BRAINSTRETCHER
TOPS. The Three Degrees and Four Tops are both singing groups.

PAGE 47

Jig-a-Link

PAGE 48

What a Pane

Fragments 7 and 10

BETWEENER
RUN

PAGE 49

Wordsearch – Collective Nouns

Bevy (quail), Brood (hens), Business (ferrets), Charm (goldfinches), Clowder (cats), Covey (partridges), Crash (rhinos), Desert (lapwings), Exaltation (larks), Flock (sheep), Gaggle (geese), Herd (cattle), Knot (toads), Murder (crows), Murmuration (starlings), Pack (wolves), Parliament (rooks), Pride (lions), Rabble (rats), School (whales), Shrewdness (apes), Spring (teal), Troop (monkeys), Unkindness (ravens), Watch (nightingales)

INITIAL REACTION
BETTER LATE THAN NEVER

PAGE 50

Find the Ships

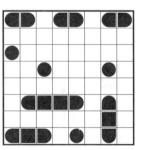

ALTER EGO
HULK HOGAN (Terry Bollea)

PAGE 51

Sudoku

4	6	7	1	2	8	3	9	5
2	9	3	6	7	5	4	8	1
1	8	5	3	9	4	2	7	6
7	2	1	4	8	3	6	5	9
9	3	8	2	5	6	1	4	7
6	5	4	9	1	7	8	2	3
8	1	6	5	4	9	7	3	2
3	7	9	8	6	2	5	1	4
5	4	2	7	3	1	9	6	8

LOGICAL
Fluffy was from London and
won the gold medal.
Fluffy, gold, London
Tabby, silver, Liverpool
Ginger, bronze, Glasgow

PAGE 52

Crossword

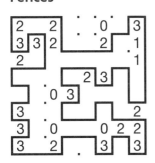

PAGE 53

Fences

ADDITION SWITCH
509 + 138 = 647

PAGE 54

Split Decisions

CHOP AND CHANGE
PELICAN (drop an N)

PAGE 55

123

2	1	3	1	2	3
1	3	2	3	1	2
3	2	1	2	3	1
1	3	2	1	2	3
2	1	3	2	3	1
3	2	1	3	1	2

SUDOKU SUM
318 + 249 = 567

PAGE 56

Skeleton Crossword

PAGE 57

Hitori

4	5	1	2	2
2	2	2	5	4
2	4	3	4	5
3	3	3	4	1
3	1	5	2	1

OPPOSITE ATTRACTION
WARM, COOL

PAGE 58

Missing Links

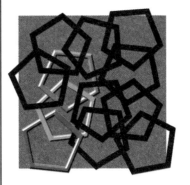

TAKE TWO
ASPECT

PAGE 59

Killer Sudoku

7	1	9	3	6	8	2	5	4
3	2	4	9	5	7	1	8	6
5	8	6	4	2	1	7	9	3
1	4	3	6	8	9	5	7	2
9	7	2	5	1	3	6	4	8
6	5	8	2	7	4	3	1	9
8	6	7	1	4	2	9	3	5
2	3	1	8	9	5	4	6	7
4	9	5	7	3	6	8	2	1

BRAINSTRETCHER
TEN. The letters of ONE are
at the centre of Indonesia; the
letters of TEN are at the centre of
Liechtenstein

PAGE 60

Dateline

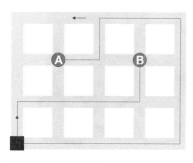

The date is 25 February 1986, when Corazon Aquino was sworn in as President of the Philippines, replacing dictator Ferdinand Marcos.

PAGE 61

One-Way Streets

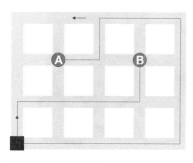

MAKE TRACKS
1 Futon 2 Clone 3 Sitar 4 Chant
5 Beret. BULLFIGHTER and MOUNTAINEER

PAGE 62

Hyper-Sudoku

9	8	2	3	5	1	7	4	6
1	7	6	2	9	4	5	8	3
4	5	3	8	6	7	9	1	2
8	9	4	1	7	3	2	6	5
7	6	5	4	2	9	8	3	1
2	3	1	5	8	6	4	9	7
5	4	8	6	3	2	1	7	9
6	2	7	9	1	8	3	5	4
3	1	9	7	4	5	6	2	8

INITIAL REACTION
A Fool and His Money Are Soon Parted

PAGE 63

Star Search

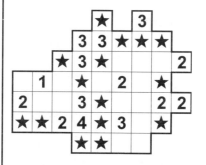

TELEPHONE TRIOS
APPEASE, COMFORT, CONSOLE

PAGE 64

Codeword

PAGE 65

ABC

CLUELESS CROSSWORD

PAGE 66

Skeleton Crossword

PAGE 67

Sudoku

4	5	3	2	6	7	9	8	1
2	9	7	1	8	4	5	6	3
8	6	1	5	3	9	2	4	7
1	3	2	7	4	8	6	9	5
7	8	9	6	5	3	4	1	2
5	4	6	9	1	2	3	7	8
6	7	5	3	9	1	8	2	4
9	2	4	8	7	5	1	3	6
3	1	8	4	2	6	7	5	9

AND SO ON
BRIGHT and EARLY

PAGE 68

Crossword

PAGE 69

Line Drawing

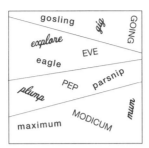

The words in each region start and end with the same letter

BETWEENER
BROOM

PAGE 70

Find the Ships

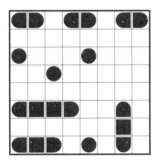

MAKE TRACKS
1 Coral 2 Adorn 3 Stork
4 Moose 5 Lever. CONDITIONER
and HAIRDRESSER

PAGE 71

Fences

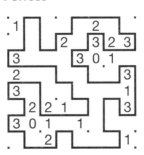

ADDITION SWITCH
516 + 291 = 807

PAGE 72

Skeleton Crossword

PAGE 73

Stamp Collection

A stamp 2,
B stamp 4,
C stamp 8

RHYMING TRIO
FAIR, HEIR, RARE

PAGE 74

123

SUDOKU SUM
408 + 129 = 537

PAGE 75

Hitori

3	4	2	4	1
5	4	5	1	3
1	4	4	3	5
2	3	1	4	4
1	1	1	2	3

OPPOSITE ATTRACTION
MORE, LESS

PAGE 76

Pathfinder – Welsh Place Names

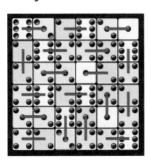

PAGE 77

Dicey Duos

INITIAL REACTION
Out of Sight Out of Mind

PAGE 78

Split Decisions

CHOP AND CHANGE
PREACH (drop the D)

PAGE 79

Hyper-Sudoku

8	2	7	3	9	5	4	6	1
4	9	3	8	1	6	5	2	7
6	5	1	4	2	7	9	8	3
9	7	6	2	5	3	1	4	8
5	1	8	6	4	9	3	7	2
2	3	4	7	8	1	6	5	9
1	6	5	9	7	2	8	3	4
3	8	2	1	6	4	7	9	5
7	4	9	5	3	8	2	1	6

AND SO ON
CHALK and CHEESE

PAGE 80

Codeword

PAGE 81

Wordsearch – Famous Artists

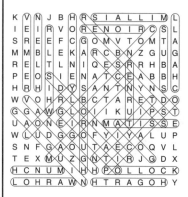

BRAINSTRETCHER
BENGALI. Castilian and Catalan are official languages of Spain and of the Spanish region of Catalonia. Hindi and Bengali are official languages of India, and its Bengal region.

PAGE 83

One-Way Streets

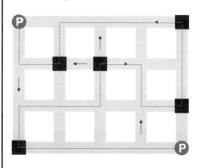

ALTER EGO
DEMI MOORE (Demetria Guynes)

PAGE 84

Crossword

PAGE 85

Pirate Ship Maze

RHYMING TRIO
BITE, RITE, TIGHT

PAGE 86

Star Search

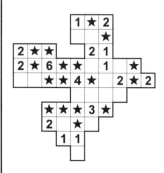

TELEPHONE TRIOS
CORSICA, OKINAWA, SUMATRA

PAGE 87

Colour In

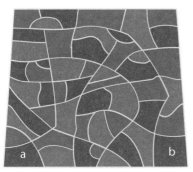

Both pieces will be blue

CHOP AND CHANGE
LEAVER (drop the S)

PAGE 88

Pieceword

S		A		K			J	A		K
S	T	O	N	I	N	G		C	U	R	R	E	N	T

(Pieceword crossword grid)

```
S A K   J A K
STONING CURRENT
O O   E C R   I E
SPAN WORDY ABET
  S     A     O
APSE FOCUS CORD
E  A L K L H  I
 TORRID REVAMP
T  T N'S P S  E
MYTH GAUNT MONK
  I     G     P
FOND PLATE STUB
B  U L R A E  L
FOOTMAN SCORING
E  Y  Y   H F
```

PAGE 89

ABC

	B	A	C
C		B	A
B	A	C	
C		A		B
A	B		C

TAKE TWO
YONDER

PAGE 90

Find the Ships

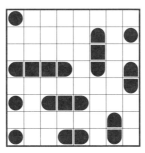

BACK NUMBERS
25

PAGE 91

Pathfinder – Printing Terms

PAGE 92

Drop Zone

N	E	T	W	O	R	K
E	T	E	R	N	A	L
C	L	I	M	A	T	E
S	O	M	E	H	O	W
T	R	A	F	F	I	C
L	A	N	T	E	R	N

P U B L I S H

BETWEENER
GREEN

PAGE 93

Sudoku

4	1	5	6	3	2	8	9	7
7	2	8	4	5	9	1	6	3
9	3	6	7	1	8	5	2	4
6	5	4	1	2	3	9	7	8
1	7	3	9	8	6	2	4	5
2	8	9	5	7	4	6	3	1
5	9	7	2	4	1	3	8	6
3	6	1	8	9	7	4	5	2
8	4	2	3	6	5	7	1	9

LOGICAL
Sue attends Spanish classes on Wednesday.
Monday, Emily, computing
Tuesday, Rita, art
Wednesday, Sue, Spanish

PAGE 94

Killer Sudoku

5	9	8	3	2	7	4	6	1
4	7	3	9	1	6	5	2	8
6	1	2	8	4	5	7	9	3
8	4	6	7	3	2	9	1	5
7	5	9	1	6	8	2	3	4
3	2	1	4	5	9	8	7	6
1	8	4	2	9	3	6	5	7
9	3	5	6	7	4	1	8	2
2	6	7	5	8	1	3	4	9

ADDITION SWITCH
193 + 286 = 479

PAGE 95

Codeword

```
JAYWALKER BLUFF
 V O  I  M W O O
SALUTE BLIZZARD
 I N   O S E  E
GLADNESS PENCIL
 E  X S   G  G
CONDUIT CAYENNE
 C   L  D   E
SCUPPER COMPERE
 U E  H P A
SPARED ATTORNEY
 A V A R  Q B
UNHARMED STUBBY
 C D P E O  E
TYPED GRATITUDE
```

S	C	K	E	I	T	Q	R	F	N	V	X	A
Z	D	G	B	M	P	O	L	Y	U	J	H	W

PAGE 96

Hitori

3	3	2	5	6	2
5	6	4	6	2	2
3	2	4	1	4	6
1	6	5	4	2	6
2	4	6	4	1	5
1	6	3	2	2	1

OPPOSITE ATTRACTION
BIG, LITTLE

PAGE 97

Hyper-Sudoku

3	7	8	5	1	9	2	4	6
1	9	6	7	4	2	3	8	5
2	5	4	8	3	6	9	1	7
6	2	3	1	8	7	4	5	9
7	4	9	3	2	5	1	6	8
5	8	1	9	6	4	7	2	3
8	3	5	4	7	1	6	9	2
4	6	7	2	9	8	5	3	1
9	1	2	6	5	3	8	7	4

MAKE TRACKS
1 Vague 2 Inter 3 Femme
4 Weary 5 Steep.
LAUNDERETTE and
SUPERMARKET

PAGE 98

Crossword

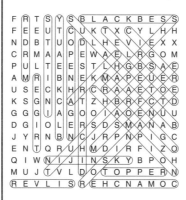

PAGE 99

Wordsearch – Horse Play

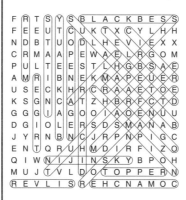

INITIAL REACTION
It Is No Use Crying over Spilt Milk

PAGE 100

Go with the Flow

ALTER EGO
MARTIN SHEEN (Ramon Estevez)

PAGE 101

Jig-a-Link

PAGE 102

One-Way Streets

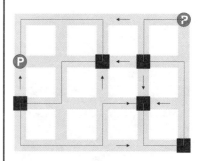

CHOP AND CHANGE
BENIGN (drop the D)

PAGE 103

123

3	1	2	3	2	1	3	2	1
2	3	1	2	1	3	2	1	3
1	2	3	1	3	2	1	3	2
3	1	2	3	2	1	3	2	1
1	3	1	2	3	2	1	3	2
3	2	3	1	2	1	2	1	3
2	1	2	3	1	3	1	3	2
1	2	3	1	3	2	3	2	1
2	3	1	2	1	3	2	1	3

SUDOKU SUM
649 + 103 = 752

PAGE 104

Line Drawing

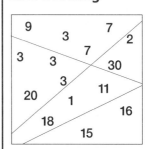

THREE OF A KIND
VANILLA ICE CREAM

PAGE 105

Number Jig

9	6	1	8	8	8	9		1	0	7	5	6	3	6
7		3		0		7	1	4		2		3		1
6	1	5	5	6		4		1	5	7	5	4	5	7
3		2		0		5	6	7		4				3
6	6	2	1	4	8	7		9	0	2	8	8	4	
	7			2		6	7	6		5		2		8
8	1	4	5	8	1	2		3	1	3	2	7	2	1
6		1		8				6			4			7
9	0	2	0	8	4	9		6	7	6	7	1	6	8
3		4		4		5	8	3		3				8
	5	2	4	7	0	1		5	2	5	0	8	8	7
2				6		1	1	0		0		7		8
1	3	3	6	4	6	2		1		9	1	2	4	1
0		6		0		7	3	2		4		8		7
7	0	8	4	8	0	7		6	6	1	8	2	7	6

PAGE 106

Star Search

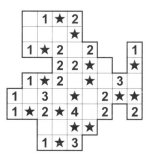

TELEPHONE TRIOS
NOTABLE, SPECIAL, UNUSUAL

PAGE 107

Tri-Colour Maze

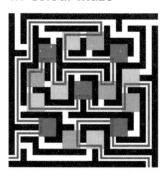

RHYMING TRIO
WOE, BLOW, DOUGH

PAGE 108

Skeleton Crossword

PAGE 109

Hyper-Sudoku

5	1	9	4	2	7	6	3	8
8	7	3	6	5	1	4	9	2
6	2	4	9	3	8	7	5	1
4	5	8	1	7	6	3	2	9
7	6	2	3	9	5	8	1	4
3	9	1	8	4	2	5	6	7
2	3	5	7	1	4	9	8	6
9	4	6	2	8	3	1	7	5
1	8	7	5	6	9	2	4	3

TAKE TWO
GAMBOL

PAGE 110

ABC

	A	B	C
C		A	B
A	B	C	
B	C		A
	A	B	C

CLUELESS CROSSWORD

S	T	E	W	A	R	D
C		N		B		E
A	R	D	U	O	U	S
L		M		L		C
L	I	O	N	I	S	E
O		S		S		N
P	O	T	S	H	O	T

PAGE 111

Codeword

M	Y	L	E	J	U	O	T	W	G	S	C	Z
B	P	I	H	K	F	Q	R	N	X	V	A	D

PAGE 112

Wheels and Cogs

Frog 1

BETWEENER
SCREW

PAGE 113

Find the Ships

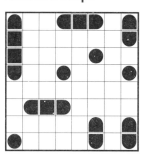

BRAINSTRETCHER
ROME. Charles de Gaulle is the main airport of Paris; Leonardo da Vinci is the main airport of Rome

PAGE 114

Triad Split Decisions

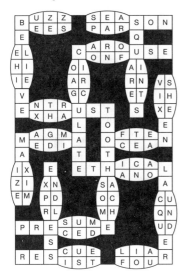

SUDOKU SUM
179 + 503 = 682

PAGE 115

Crossword

PAGE 116

123

1	3	1	2	3	2	3	1	2
2	1	2	3	1	3	1	2	3
3	2	3	1	2	1	3	1	2
2	3	1	2	1	3	2	3	1
3	1	2	1	3	2	1	2	3
1	2	3	2	1	3	2	3	1
2	3	1	3	2	1	3	1	2
1	2	3	1	3	2	1	2	3
3	1	2	3	2	1	2	3	1

CHOP AND CHANGE
PICASSO (drop the U)

PAGE 117

Fences

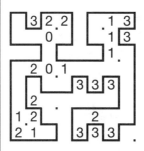

ADDITION SWITCH
384 + 192 = 576

PAGE 118

Alphabetical Crossword

PAGE 119

Mask Maze

LOGICAL
Newcastle played Fulham
at 15:00.
13:30, West Ham, Hull City
15:00, Fulham, Newcastle
17:15, Chelsea, Aston Villa

PAGE 121

Wordsearch – Eye of the Tiger

The extra word is STRIPES

LOOK HEAR
PIQUE, PEAK, PEEK

PAGE 122

Hyper-Sudoku

6	4	8	9	3	5	1	7	2
2	5	1	6	8	7	4	9	3
7	3	9	2	4	1	5	8	6
9	8	4	7	5	6	2	3	1
5	2	7	3	1	4	9	6	8
1	6	3	8	2	9	7	4	5
8	7	5	4	6	2	3	1	9
3	9	2	1	7	8	6	5	4
4	1	6	5	9	3	8	2	7

MAKE TRACKS
1 Imbue 2 Snuff 3 Vital
4 Later 5 Petty.
EMANCIPATED and
SUFFRAGETTE

PAGE 123

Pieceword

PAGE 124

One-Way Streets

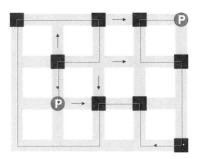

TAKE TWO
STUPOR

PAGE 125

Star Search

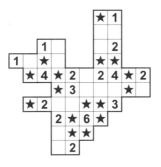

TELEPHONE TRIOS
CHATEAU, COTTAGE, MANSION

PAGE 126

Crossword

PAGE 127

Sets of Three

AND SO ON
BREAD and JAM

PAGE 128

Sudoku

9	2	1	5	3	6	4	7	8
6	7	8	2	4	9	3	5	1
5	4	3	8	1	7	9	6	2
3	5	2	6	8	1	7	4	9
4	8	9	7	5	2	6	1	3
7	1	6	3	9	4	8	2	5
2	3	4	1	6	8	5	9	7
8	9	7	4	2	5	1	3	6
1	6	5	9	7	3	2	8	4

BACK NUMBERS
13

PAGE 129

Look Both Ways Crossword

To the right 1 Lioness 2 Art
3 Tins 4 Foe 5 Crystal 6 Caned
7 Row 9 Doe 11 Psyche
13 Grades 14 Sea 16 Tic
19 Slipper 21 Elation 24 Flair
26 Rap 28 Twit 29 Lip 31 Tan
33 And.
To the left 2 Aid 3 Troop
4 Fitness 5 Con 6 Crests 7 Ray
8 Consign 10 Wet 12 Data
15 Yes 17 Lid 18 Calf
20 Despair 22 Certain 23 Letter
25 Ill 27 Saint 30 Pip 32 War
34 Pod.

PAGE 130

Split Decisions

CHOP AND CHANGE
CRANIUM (drop the E)

PAGE 131

Hitori

5	6	1	6	3	5
4	5	5	6	1	5
5	2	6	6	4	3
3	3	3	4	2	6
2	6	4	5	3	1
3	4	2	1	6	4

OPPOSITE ATTRACTION
MESSY, NEAT

PAGE 132

Number Jig

4	0	6	9		5	1	5	7	6		5	3	3	1
3			2	2	4		6		7			2		5
6	6	7	0		4	7	7	5	3	6		7		2
7			7		6		8			1	2	1	9	8
		8	3	7	3		9	3	6	8			4	
8	2	0		2		8		0		8	6	7	7	5
3		3		1	0	7	0	8	7			7		0
4	3	0	2	6		6		3		4	5	0	5	3
5		1			8	1	8	3	1	1		6		4
3	8	5	7	3		1		6		0		3	3	5
	4			1	0	8	1		8	0	5	7		
2	7	9	2	6			2		1		4			7
3		7		6	6	4	2	5	1		2	6	6	8
3		4			2		0		3	7	3			7
6	2	8	1		8	4	2	4	6		3	4	1	7

PAGE 133

ABC

A | C | B
A | C | B | |
C | B | A | |
  | | C | B | A
B | | | A | C

CLUELESS CROSSWORD

S E L L E R S
E | I | D | L
I N Q U I R Y
Z | U | F | N
I T E M I S E
N | F | C | S
G E Y S E R S

PAGE 134

Shadow Play

Image 4

BETWEENER
BOOK

PAGE 135

Line Drawing

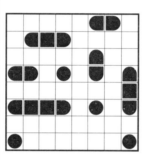

The top region has four pairs of homophones (words that sound the same but are spelled differently), the words in the middle region are palindromes (they read the same backwards and forwards), and the bottom region has five pairs of words that spell each other in reverse.

THREE OF A KIND
LIVE AND LEARN

PAGE 136

Skeleton Crossword

PAGE 137

Find the Ships

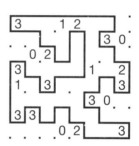

ALTER EGO
DANNY DEVITO (Daniel Michaeli)

PAGE 138

Hyper-Sudoku

8 3 5 1 2 7 9 4 6
6 2 7 5 9 4 1 8 3
1 9 4 3 8 6 5 2 7
5 1 6 8 4 9 3 7 2
4 7 9 6 3 2 8 5 1
3 8 2 7 1 5 4 6 9
7 6 1 4 5 3 2 9 8
2 5 3 9 6 8 7 1 4
9 4 8 2 7 1 6 3 5

INITIAL REACTION
Many a True Word Is Spoken in Jest

PAGE 139

Codeword

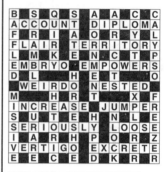

Z E L N K A Q X I M R Y H
D C S B O T U P G V J F W

PAGE 140

Fences

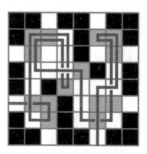

ADDITION SWITCH
617 + 237 = 854

PAGE 141

Straight Ahead

BRAINSTRETCHER
TETHYS. Europa and Callisto are moons of Jupiter; Titan and Tethys are moons of Saturn

Hitori

OPPOSITE ATTRACTION
ANGRY, CALM

Honeycomb Crossword

1 Manage 2 Acting 3 Remove
4 Meagre 5 Ignite 6 Detour 7 Planet
8 Calmer 9 Negate 10 Gimlet
11 Driver 12 Revise 13 Menace
14 Credit 15 Encode 16 Almond
17 Ignore 18 Robber 19 Caress
20 Tinder 21 Docile 22 Dahlia
23 Region 24 Nobble 25 Lesson
26 Nicked 27 Decide 28 Haggle
29 Bigger 30 Select 31 Canoes
32 Seeker 33 Deface 34 Feeler
35 Tribal 36 Lasted 37 Across
38 Relate 39 Casual 40 Create
41 Tartan 42 Sudden 43 Morsel
44 Settee 45 Campus 46 Access
47 Snared 48 Duster 49 Tackle
50 Madcap 51 Spoils 52 Droops
53 Adapts 54 Pliant.

Pathfinder – Tool Kit

SUDOKU SUM
125 + 739 = 864

Killer Sudoku

3	1	6	7	8	2	9	4	5
9	7	4	3	5	1	2	8	6
5	8	2	9	6	4	3	1	7
2	9	5	4	7	6	1	3	8
7	3	8	1	2	5	6	9	4
6	4	1	8	3	9	5	7	2
4	5	7	2	9	3	8	6	1
1	6	9	5	4	8	7	2	3
8	2	3	6	1	7	4	5	9

CLUELESS CROSSWORD

123

3	1	2	3	1	2	1	3	2
1	2	3	1	2	3	2	1	3
2	3	1	2	3	2	1	3	1
1	2	3	1	2	1	3	2	3
3	1	2	3	1	3	2	1	2
2	3	1	2	3	2	1	3	1
1	2	3	1	2	1	3	2	3
3	1	2	3	1	3	2	1	2
2	3	1	2	3	1	3	2	1

BETWEENER
ROAD

Wordsearch – Creepy Crawlies

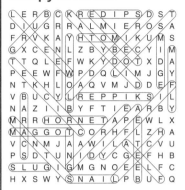

BACK NUMBERS
49

Looped Path

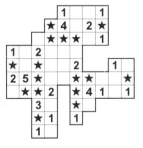

RHYMING TRIO
JOT, SPOT, WHAT

Star Search

TELEPHONE TRIOS
DUCTILE, ELASTIC, PLIABLE

PAGE 150

All in One Crossword

A	D	V		A		E	S		S	
N	O	I	S	E	S		P	R	O	M	P	T	L	Y
G		S		M		D		I		R		M
O	P	P	O	R	T	U	N	E		T	R	A	M	P
R		E		S		N				T		T
A	C	R	O	B	A	T		T	O	R	N	A	D	O
		S		A		E		I				M
S	W	E	A	T	E	R		S	P	O	U	S	E	S
O				H				O		T		E
R	E	P	R	E	S	S		M	A	S	S	A	G	E
C		R				O		B		E		Y
E	R	A	S	E		F	O	R	M	U	L	A	T	E
R		Y		L		T		E		P		G	I
E	L	E	V	A	T	E	D		G	O	B	L	I	N
R		R		N		N		N				E	N	G

PAGE 151

Sudoku

1	9	7	2	3	8	5	4	6
3	5	8	1	4	6	7	2	9
6	2	4	9	5	7	1	3	8
2	1	9	3	6	5	8	7	4
7	4	3	8	9	1	2	6	5
5	8	6	7	2	4	3	9	1
9	7	1	4	8	3	6	5	2
4	3	5	6	1	2	9	8	7
8	6	2	5	7	9	4	1	3

MAKE TRACKS
1 Wager 2 Shade 3 Amber
4 Stock 5 Screw.
MATHEMATICS and HEAD
TEACHER

PAGE 152

One-Way Streets

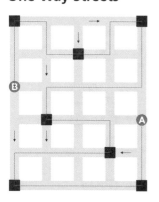

TAKE TWO
MUSTER

PAGE 153

ABC

C	A			B	
B			C		A
A		B			C
	C	A			B
	B	C	A		

AND SO ON
FUSS and BOTHER

PAGE 154

Crossword

U		P		A		E		S		T		L		P
S	L	I	P	P	E	D	U	P		O	S	I	E	R
A		R		E		I		R		X		Q		E
G	U	I	L	D		S	P	I	R	I	T	U	A	L
E		P		O		N		C		O		U		
	V	I	R	G	I	N		T	O	W	E	R	E	D
	R		A			E		A						E
D	I	S	I	N	T	E	R	E	S	T	E	D		
F		N		O		T		C						
I	N	T	E	G	E	R		C	H	E	E	S	Y	
T		R		R		T		I		T		A		A
T	R	I	C	O	L	O	U	R		G	U	A	R	D
I		F		U		I		C		R		T		A
N	Y	L	O	N		S	Q	U	E	A	L	I	N	G
G		E		D		E	S	M		C	E			

PAGE 155

Killer Sudoku

2	9	7	5	3	1	4	8	6
1	4	6	2	8	9	5	3	7
8	3	5	6	4	7	9	2	1
5	8	1	9	7	4	2	6	3
7	6	3	8	5	2	1	4	9
9	2	4	1	6	3	8	7	5
6	5	9	7	2	8	3	1	4
3	7	8	4	1	5	6	9	2
4	1	2	3	9	6	7	5	8

BETWEENER
TEA

PAGE 156

Find the Ships

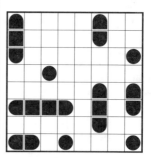

BRAINSTRETCHER
ABEL MAGWITCH. Nancy and
Mr Bumble are characters from
Dickens' *Oliver Twist*; Pip and
Abel Magwitch are from *Great
Expectations*

PAGE 157

123

2	3	1	2	3	1	2	1	3
3	1	2	3	1	2	3	2	1
1	2	3	1	2	3	1	3	2
3	1	2	3	1	2	3	2	1
1	2	3	1	2	3	2	1	3
3	1	2	3	1	2	1	3	2
2	3	1	2	3	1	2	1	3
1	2	3	1	2	3	1	3	2
2	3	1	2	3	1	3	2	1

SUDOKU SUM
216 + 489 = 705

PAGE 159

Number Jig

1	5	0	8		4	0	9	2	1		2	7	3	7
3			9	2	5		0		2		7		1	
4	6	2	3		5	0	6	1	0	4		4		1
1			0		6		8			6	7	4	7	6
		8	4	3	1		2	9	4	3		5		
6	3	6		8		8		3		8	0	5	3	8
3		8		1	8	6	7	8	6			3		0
2	0	2	3	3		6		5		8	4	7	2	8
8	7			5	1	1	7	5	5		7		2	
9	5	6	5	5		8		0		1		7	0	4
	8			9	4	3	7		3	3	6	2		
8	0	2	4	8			1		2		7			5
5		2		2	1	3	8	6	8		5	1	0	3
4		8			7		5		2	1	1		6	
8	4	8	8		6	2	0	4	6		5	2	0	0

PAGE 160

Fences

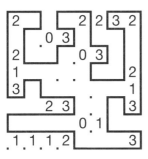

ADDITION SWITCH
193 + 475 = 668

PAGE 161

Hitori

1	5	1	6	2	3
2	6	6	6	4	3
5	1	4	2	4	6
6	5	2	5	5	1
3	6	4	4	1	2
5	4	1	3	6	4

OPPOSITE ATTRACTION
REVEAL, HIDE

PAGE 162

Roundabout Crossword

Radial: Inwards 1 Sword 4 Acted
5 Horse 6 Prose 7 Acute 8 Baste
10 Epees 13 Litre 15 Unite
16 Crate 17 Safer 18 Enter
19 Piper 21 Tryst 22 Feast 23 Ingot
24 Robot.
Radial: Outwards 2 Drone
3 Desks 9 Seems 11 Salon
12 Saint 14 Error 20 Ready.
Circular: Clockwise 7 Absent
22 Firs 26 Camp 27 Onion
29 Renown 30 Rouse 35 Boost
36 Ear 37 Tee 38 Sorest 39 Desert.
Circular: Anticlockwise 6 Phase
16 Curl 21 Types 25 Rock 28 Dinar
31 Tile 32 Fair 33 Apt 34 Gay.

PAGE 163

Farm Maze

BETWEENER
METER

PAGE 164

Hyper-Sudoku

8	2	7	9	3	1	6	4	5
5	1	6	4	2	8	9	7	3
4	3	9	7	6	5	2	1	8
1	8	5	2	9	4	3	6	7
9	6	4	8	7	3	5	2	1
2	7	3	1	5	6	4	8	9
7	4	2	5	8	9	1	3	6
3	9	8	6	1	2	7	5	4
6	5	1	3	4	7	8	9	2

ALTER EGO
TINA TURNER (Annie Mae
Bullock)

PAGE 165

Wordsearch – Cultural Cities

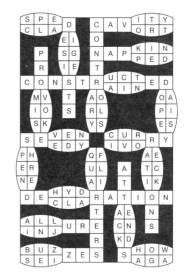

INITIAL REACTION
Too Many Cooks Spoil the Broth

PAGE 166

Anagram Crossword

PAGE 167

Triad Split Decisions

CHOP AND CHANGE
STURGEON (drop the Y)

PAGE 168

One-Way Streets

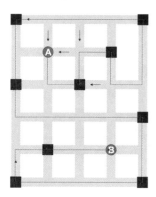

LOOK HEAR
RAISE, RAYS, RAZE

PAGE 169

Jig-a-Link

C	O	N	C	E	D	E		G	A	S		E	N	V	E	L	O	P
O		A	N		M	R		A		N		O		O		R	
P	A	N	I	C		B	O	O	T	L	E	G		T	A	B	O	O
I			O		A		T	U		O		I				U	
O	N	W	A	R	D	S		T		K		R	E	N	E	W	E	D
U		I		E		S	T	O	R	I	N	G		G		O		L
S	O	D	A		Y		A		E				P	U	N	Y	
	E	U	R	O		S	N	I	F	F		F	A	I	L	
S	O	N	G		L		T		D	R		I		O	D	D	S
P			M	E	D	I	U	M		B	A	T	E	A	U		A
A	C	H	E		E		F	O	U	N			N		S	W	A	G
	A	N	O	N		F	U	M	E	D		D	E	L	I	
B	U	S	T		M		E		E			E		Y	E	L	L
A		T		S		U	R	A	N	I	U	M		C		A	
T	R	E	A	T	E	D		F		N		B	L	U	N	D	E	R
T		A		D		R		S		R		C				G	
I	N	T	E	R		I	N	E	R	T	I	A		K	N	A	V	E
N		E		E		E		S		E		C		O		G		L
G	R	A	N	D	E	R		H	O	P		E	C	O	N	O	M	Y

PAGE 170

Colour Paths

AND SO ON
WARM and SUNNY

PAGE 171

Star Search

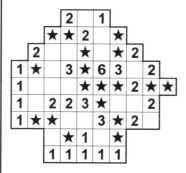

TELEPHONE TRIOS
BECKHAM, HOCKNEY,
PUTTNAM (famous Davids)

PAGE 172

Sudoku

1	2	4	8	6	3	9	5	7
6	3	9	7	5	4	8	1	2
7	8	5	2	9	1	4	6	3
9	6	1	5	2	8	7	3	4
4	7	8	3	1	6	2	9	5
2	5	3	9	4	7	1	8	6
5	4	6	1	7	9	3	2	8
8	1	2	4	3	5	6	7	9
3	9	7	6	8	2	5	4	1

THREE OF A KIND
STIR IT UP

PAGE 173

Continuity Crossword

Across 1 Scent, met, salts 2 Code, regal, meek 3 Ordeal, oboe, May 4 Ray, die, sew, numb 5 Clop, tea, red, Rio 6 Havoc, trawl, ode 7 Slash, his, eager 8 Ill, tease, rural 9 Tyre, field, deli 10 Emerald, aid, dog 11 Map, area, brooch 12 Alec, cadet, slat 13 Tiles, Sol, yells.

Down 1 Scorch, site, mat 2 Coral, ally, Mali 3 Eddy, oval, repel 4 Need, poster, ace 5 Trait, chef, arcs 6 Melee, Thai, leas 7 Egos, arise, dado 8 Tab, erase, label 9 Slow, ewer, dirty 10 Amend, laud, dose 11 Lemur, ogre, doll 12 Team, idea, local 13 Sky, Boer, lights.

PAGE 174

ABC

B	C		A		
C			A	B	
	A			B	C
	B	A	C		
A	C	B			

CLUELESS CROSSWORD

I	N	K	W	E	L	L
N		I		P		E
R	O	L	L	I	N	G
O		L		C		E
A	D	J	O	U	R	N
D		O		R		D
S	H	Y	N	E	S	S

PAGE 175

Find the Ships

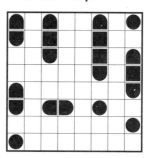

TAKE TWO
ADROIT

PAGE 176

Numerical Crossword

1	1	5	6		2	8	9		1	2	7	1
8	1	6		8	5		1	9		6	8	0
2	0	7	8	2			6	1	7	0	9	
3			8	0	9	2		4	9	2	0		8
	4	9	8		6	7	9		2	2	2	
3	8		8	7	6		4	8	4		6	4
0			4			2		1			0
6	9		4	8	3		1	6	3		1	7
	4	1	6		1	0	2		3	4	3	
5		3	2	6	4		1	2	5	6		3
6	3	5	3	2			8	3	4	9	1	
7	7	7		4	7		6	5		4	4	8
8	6	9	7		6	2	8		1	4	5	3

PAGE 177

Patchwork

Patch 3

RHYMING TRIO
CURD, HERD, THIRD

PAGE 178

123

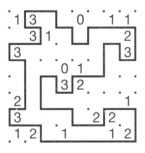

1	3	2	3	1	2	3	1	2
2	1	3	1	2	3	1	2	3
3	2	1	2	3	1	2	3	1
1	3	2	3	1	2	3	1	2
2	1	3	1	2	3	1	2	3
3	2	1	2	3	1	2	3	1
1	3	2	1	2	3	1	2	3
2	1	3	2	3	1	2	3	1
3	2	1	3	1	2	3	1	2

SUDOKU SUM
709 + 153 = 862

PAGE 179

Fences

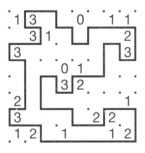

BRAINSTRETCHER
DNIEPER. The Nile and Rhône flow into the Mediterranean Sea; the Danube and Dnieper flow into the Black Sea

PAGE 180

Cryptic Crossword

PAGE 181

Hyper-Sudoku

4	7	9	6	3	1	2	5	8
6	1	8	7	5	2	3	4	9
3	5	2	9	4	8	6	1	7
1	4	6	3	8	7	5	9	2
7	8	5	2	1	9	4	3	6
2	9	3	5	6	4	7	8	1
5	2	7	8	9	3	1	6	4
8	6	4	1	7	5	9	2	3
9	3	1	4	2	6	8	7	5

ADDITION SWITCH
216 + 372 = 588

PAGE 182

Split Decisions

CHOP AND CHANGE
BULGARIAN (drop the Y)

PAGE 183

Crossword

PAGE 184

Solitaire Poker

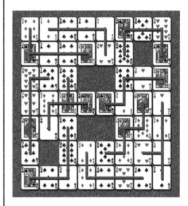

PAGE 185

Hitori

4	6	5	3	2	5
3	3	6	5	4	5
5	3	5	1	4	4
2	3	3	5	6	5
6	5	4	6	3	2
1	1	4	4	5	4

OPPOSITE ATTRACTION
ADD, SUBTRACT

PAGE 186

One-Way Streets

BACK NUMBERS
77

PAGE 187

Pieceword

F	S	K			F	S	A
F	L	E	E	I	N	G	G	L	O	W	I	N	G

FLEEING GLOWING
OPEN TAWNY TWIG
SMOG CYNIC CORM
TWELVE KINDLY
BLED RATED TINT
CAFE DOILY SKIP
POLECAT PULSATE

PAGE 188

Sudoku

1	4	5	3	8	6	7	9	2
3	6	7	9	4	2	1	8	5
9	2	8	5	1	7	3	6	4
8	9	1	7	2	3	5	4	6
5	3	6	4	9	1	2	7	8
4	7	2	6	5	8	9	1	3
7	5	4	8	3	9	6	2	1
2	8	9	1	6	5	4	3	7
6	1	3	2	7	4	8	5	9

ALTER EGO
BRUCE LEE (Lee Yuen Kam)

PAGE 189

Star Search

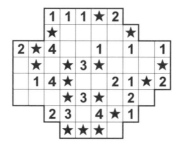

TELEPHONE TRIOS
FENCING, JAVELIN, SHOT-PUT

PAGE 190

Codeword

PAGE 191

Go with the Flow

INITIAL REACTION
Practise What You Preach

PAGE 192

Jigsaw

A, C, G and H

MAKE TRACKS
1 Fever 2 Elegy 3 Carat 4 Place
5 Snood. KEELHAULING and
WEIGH ANCHOR

PAGE 193

ABC

C	A	B		
B		A	C	
A			B	C
	C		A	B
	B	C		A

CLUELESS CROSSWORD

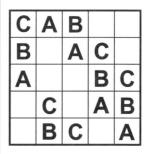

PAGE 195

Crossword

MACE DISTRAUGHT
NASAL INTESTATE
FRONTIER CRATER
SCION COOLNESS
SEASONAL ADAIR
ANTRIM CONFUSED
LONGFACED AFOOT
ABOVEBOARD VEER

PAGE 196

Find the Ships

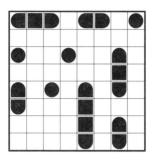

AND SO ON
FAST and FURIOUS

PAGE 197

Hyper-Sudoku

BETWEENER
FEVER

PAGE 198

Skeleton Crossword

I	S	I	S		S	O	B		R	I	T	E	
E		T		W		P		A		I	O	R	
C	H	A	P	A	T	I		N	I	G	E	R	I	A
H		R		Y		N		G		A	R	F	
O	A	T	H		S	N	A	K	E		D	E	F	T
		U		E		E		O		S		N	
J	U	P	I	T	E	R		K	I	N	E	T	I	C
U		U			U		A			O	
T	R	O	D	D	E	N		S	C	R	A	W	N	Y
	V		E		O		U		L		I	
P	I	E	D		I	M	A	G	O		A	T	O	M
A	R		S	I		A		O		H		A	
V	A	T	I	C	A	N		R	E	D	W	O	O	D
E		L		A		E		I		U		E	
	H	Y	M	N		L	I	D		N	O	T	E	

PAGE 199

Killer Sudoku

9	8	3	4	7	1	6	5	2
2	6	4	3	9	5	1	7	8
5	1	7	6	2	8	9	3	4
7	3	1	5	8	6	2	4	9
8	4	5	2	1	9	7	6	3
6	2	9	7	4	3	8	1	5
3	5	8	9	6	7	4	2	1
4	9	6	1	3	2	5	8	7
1	7	2	8	5	4	3	9	6

RHYMING TRIO
SOAK, SPOKE, YOLK

PAGE 200

Fences

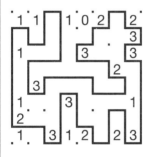

ADDITION SWITCH
305 + 179 = 484

PAGE 201

First Thoughts

D		F		L		P		U		D		S	
O	N	E	W	A	Y		M	I	S	S	P	E	N	T
R		E		V		S		C		E		V		A
S	A	L	V	A	T	I	O	N		R	E	I	G	N
A		G			N		I			L		D	
L	O	O	K	I	N	G		C	H	E	L	S	E	A
		R		L			L			R	
B	E	D	T	I	M	E		R	E	D	U	C	E	D
A			S			E		E		O	
L	E	A	T	H	E	R		C	E	R	A	M	I	C
L		L		E		O		P		A	
R	O	L	L	S		F	U	R	N	I	T	U	R	E
O		I		U		D		C		T		S	
O	P	E	N	C	A	S	T		G	E	N	E	V	A
M		D		K		E		D		R		R	

PAGE 202

123

1	2	3	2	3	1	3	2	1
2	3	1	3	1	2	1	3	2
1	2	3	1	2	1	3	2	3
2	1	2	3	1	3	2	3	1
3	2	3	1	2	1	3	1	2
1	3	1	2	3	2	1	2	3
3	1	2	3	1	3	2	1	2
2	3	1	2	3	2	1	3	1
3	1	2	1	2	3	2	1	3

SUDOKU SUM
147 + 362 = 509

PAGE 203

Hitori

5	6	1	6	3	2
2	1	2	5	2	3
6	6	2	1	4	5
1	5	2	2	2	4
5	2	4	1	1	6
2	3	5	6	2	3

OPPOSITE ATTRACTION
COSTLY, CHEAP

PAGE 204

Codeword

```
S S B H D S T S
P R E M A T U R E   P L E A T
A Q I N R R X I
S K U L L   G R A V Y   T O R
M E I L U
  U L N A   C E L L U L O S E
A M U N O W
B E S P O K E   T R I C K L E
L E U U F
E N D O R S I N G   Y O L K
A A N I B
J O T   W A F E R   G R A Z E
I E H E A H I R
V A L V E   S U C C E S S O R
E Y T T E E Y
```

```
S T A W J R C I M K O Y D
E L N Z H V G U F B P X Q
```

PAGE 205

Wordsearch – 60s & 70s Bands

CHOP AND CHANGE
GRANDEE (drop one D)

PAGE 206

Turn Maze

ALTER EGO
WOODY ALLEN
(Allen Konigsberg)

PAGE 207

Crossword

```
D I S C L A I M   H A C K E D
E A E L W H A
R E C E N T L Y   B E C A L M
R R I T B S K A
I M A G E   R E A S O N I N G
C M N E N E A
K E E P T R A C K   E R S E
N T E P
  S T U D   M U R D E R O U S
A I E S X O P
C R E S C E N D O   P I N T O
C L T T R L B R
O R D A I N   I D E A L I S T
S E O E I L E
T I R A N A   B R I N D L E D
```

PAGE 208

ABCD

THREE OF A KIND
GOING FOR GOLD

PAGE 209

Sudoku

```
5 8 7 9 3 4 6 2 1
4 2 1 8 6 5 9 7 3
9 3 6 7 1 2 5 8 4
1 6 8 2 5 3 7 4 9
7 5 9 1 4 8 2 3 6
3 4 2 6 9 7 1 5 8
2 1 5 3 8 6 4 9 7
6 7 3 4 2 9 8 1 5
8 9 4 5 7 1 3 6 2
```

BRAINSTRETCHER
WATER. A perch extends into the air; a jetty extends into the water

PAGE 210

Pieceword

```
S E C U R E D   C H I M P
S E O E U A N E
O R G A N Z A   S I D E C A R
L M T P T I S
O V E R R I P E   C H A S T E
N O R P U E V
R E T A L I A T E   M I D G E
E L I R I
M U F T I   S E P U L C H R E
I L N E E I O
T W I N G E   S T E A L I N G
P P S U T S I
I M P R I N T   A V I A T O R
N E V E T O E L
G I D D Y   P R E E N E D
```

PAGE 211

One-Way Streets

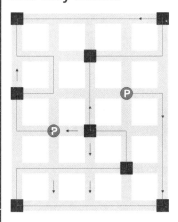

INITIAL REACTION
There's No Place Like Home

PAGE 212

Killer Sudoku

```
2 5 6 1 3 7 4 8 9
4 9 1 2 8 6 5 3 7
8 3 7 5 9 4 6 2 1
9 1 5 7 4 2 3 6 8
3 7 2 8 6 1 9 4 5
6 4 8 3 5 9 7 1 2
5 6 3 9 2 8 1 7 4
1 2 4 6 7 5 8 9 3
7 8 9 4 1 3 2 5 6
```

CHOP AND CHANGE
SCIMITAR (drop the E)

PAGE 213

Codeword

```
D E P O S E   A M U S I N G
E   E   I   C   A   L   O   B
S T R E T C H E R   A M B L E
I   F   A   O   Q   N   L   R
S C O U R   S O U N D N E S S
T   R   E   E   E   E
  E M I N E N C E   R O V E R
J   E   E   U   E   E   K
U D D E R   B R O O D I N G
N     V   E       D   T   W
I N S P E C T E D   F A I T H
P   P   L   W   I   R   L   E
E L I T E   E X T R I C A T E
R   R   S   E   Y   A   T   Z
  P E R S O N A   B R E E Z E
```

```
W L M Y G T U V C B R F A
I X P N Q H O D Z S J K E
```

PAGE 214

T-Rex Maze

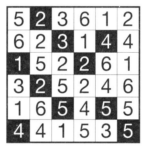

LOOK HEAR
BRAZE, BRAISE, BRAYS

PAGE 215

Star Search

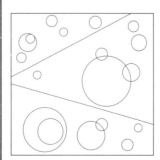

TELEPHONE TRIOS
SUCCESS, TRIUMPH, VICTORY

PAGE 216

Jig-a-Link

```
T R A G I C   L E E C H   M I D G E T
E   I   U   O   A   A   O   A     A
T   S H R E W   R   V A U N T     W
H A L T   A   E N N U I   L   A C I D
E   E   C O S   N O D   O   R
R E A L L Y   T Y I N G   Y E A R L Y
  P   E   T   G   A
B A T H E D   G L E A M   C O O L E D
R   E   A R M I L   F   O
I D O L   I B I S   A N T I   F O R M
E   L   S   E   E   E   M   A   E
F E L O N Y   F A C E D   B E L T E D
  A   A   R   A   I
B O D E G A   S L U M P   M U G G E D
E   E   I R A   A L E   H   E
H I N T   R   L I K E N   L   S T A B
E   H O I S T E   T I L D E   T
L   U   L   E   E   E   O   L   O
D E A D L Y   D I N E D   W I L D E R
```

PAGE 217

Hitori

OPPOSITE ATTRACTION
PLAIN, ORNATE

PAGE 218

Line Drawing

BETWEENER
CARPET

PAGE 219

Crossword

```
A B D U C T E D   S C R I P
  I   G   R   U   A   E   O
R E G A L I A   B A N E F U L
O   H   I   I   C   D   I   Y
Y V E S   P N E U M A T I C
A   A   P   S   K   A     H
L A D D E R E D   A R B O U R
A   E   C   D   L   T   X   O
I N D O C K   N I H I L I S M
R   A   T   L   N   D   A
F I R E D R I L L   L I F T
O   U   I   S   I   I S   I
R O M U L U S   P O N T I A C
C   B   L   U   U   C   N
E R A T O   E S T R A N G E
```

PAGE 220

Triad Split Decisions

CHOP AND CHANGE
RECEPTIONIST (drop the V)

Extra Starter Letters
Here are some extra starters
for the harder codewords in
the volume.

Codeword first starter hint
p95: 15 = D
p111: 8 = T
p139: 11 = R
p190: 14 = T
p204: 8 = I
p213: 10 = B
Codeword second starter hint
p204: 15 = L
p213: 20 = O

INDIGO EDITION

Published in the United Kingdom by Vivat Direct Limited (t/a Reader's Digest), 157 Edgware Road, London W2 2HR

Mindstretchers is owned and under licence from The Reader's Digest Association, Inc. All rights reserved.

Produced by Puzzler Media Limited, Redhill, for Vivat Direct Limited (t/a Reader's Digest)

FOR PUZZLER MEDIA
Volume editor George Rankin
Designer Wilson Hui

FOR VIVAT DIRECT
Project editor Christine Noble

Editorial director Julian Browne
Art director Anne-Marie Bulat
Managing editor Nina Hathway
Picture resource manager Sarah Stewart-Richardson
Pre-press technical manager Dean Russell
Product production manager Claudette Bramble
Production controller Sandra Fuller

Printing and binding Arvato Iberia, Portugal

ISBN: 978 0 276 44562 0
BOOK CODE: 643-005 UP0000-3
ORACLE CODE: 355600018S.00.24
CONCEPT CODE: US 4967/L